Home Remedies

Dr. Rekha Deshpandey

Deshpandey, Dr. Rekha
Home Remedies

© *Publisher*
ISBN 978-1-905863-12-9

First edition 2008

Published by
ibs BOOKS (UK)
55, Warren Street, London W1T 5NW
email: sales@ibsbooks.co.uk
www.ibsbooks.co.uk

Printed in India at
Star Print O Bind
New Delhi

Book Designed at
i-Links 'n' Grafix
New Delhi

All rights reserved. No part of this publication may be reproduced, stored in a retrieval system, or transmitted in any way or by any means, electronic, mechanical, photocopying, recording or otherwise, without the prior written permission of the publisher.

Contents

Acidity	5	Cervical Spondylosis	44
Acne	8	Chickenpox	45
Age Spots	10	Common Cold/Flu	47
Alcoholism/Cirrhosis of Liver	12	Conjunctivitis	49
Amnesia/Loss ofMemory	14	Constipation	51
Anorexia	16	Corns	53
Appendicitis	18	Cough/Sore Throat	55
Arteriosclerosis	19	Dandruff	58
Arthritis	21	Dark Complexion/Sunburn	60
Asthma	24	Dark Underarms	63
Athlete's Foot	27	Depression	64
Backache	29	Diabetes	65
Bad Breath	31	Diarrhoea	67
Bites/Stings	33	Dry or Oily Skin	70
Body Odour	35	Ear Infection	73
Boils	37	Eczema	75
Bronchitis	39	Fever	77
Bruises	41	Gum Trouble	79
Burns	42	Hair Problems	80

Headache	83
Hiccups	86
High Blood Pressure/Hypertension	88
Insomnia	90
Peptic Ulcers	92
Skin Rash	94
Stomach Pain/Indigestion	95
Varicose Veins	97
Warts	99
Worms	101

Female Problems

Anaemia	104
Bacterial Vaginitis	106
Breast Feeding	108
Female Infertility	110
Frigidity	112
Leucorrhoea	113
Menopause	115
Menstruation	117
Oedema/Water Retention	119
Pregnancy Problems	121

Male Problems

Erectile Dysfunction	124
Prostate Enlargement	126

1

Acidity

This is a common problem among middle-aged men and women. Overeating or binging can lead to a burning sensation behind the breastbone and at times, in the stomach. At the same time, one may witness salty or sore gastric contents or bitter greenish yellow bile rise up to the mouth. The unease and discomfort may also extend to the neck and occasionally to the upper arms. A number of eatables, like hot, spicy and fried food, strong chocolates, garlic, onions, cigarettes, prolonged medication and intake of drinks like alcohol, excessive tea, or coffee, or smoking, can set it in. Even excessive exposure to the sun can lead to hyperacidity. Stress-related situations that cause anger, fear or worry can aggravate the condition.

Normally acidity or 'heartburn', as it is often referred to, occurs when hydrochloric acid, an important ingredient of digestive juices, makes its way upward to enter the food-pipe from the stomach. It is said that the oesophageal sphincter that lies between the food-pipe and the stomach, on irritation of the food-pipe, can incite the problem. Vomiting and headache are also some of the symptoms of acidity.

 Precautions

- Stop or lower the intake of coffee, tea and colas as they cause the acid to rise up.
- Avoid tobacco and alcohol as far as possible.
- Increase the intake of water so that it neutralises the effect of hydrochloric acid.
- Do not go to bed immediately after a meal. Go for a walk or stay awake for two to three hours before sleeping.
- Resist taking heavy meals containing excess of refined flour, sweets and meat.
- Keep away from spicy food.
- Avoid hot spicy foods.

Precautions

- Medicines, like aspirin or certain antibiotics, antidepressants and sedatives may aggravate the burning feeling in the stomach.
- Avoid beans, cabbage, Brussel's sprouts, cauliflower, onion, radish and banana as these cause gas formation.

Home Remedies

- Try sleeping on the left side as the fluids flow away from the oesophageal sphincter.
- Take plenty of fluids — a minimum of six to eight glasses of water. While any fluid is good, water is the elixir of life. It will wash the acid back down the oesophagus into the stomach.
- Eat lots of green vegetables and fruits.
- Replace white bread with brown wheat bread.
- Go for long walks.
- Wear loose-fitting clothes.
- Drink cold milk twice a day by sipping it slowly.
- A decoction of *chandan* (sandalwood powder) may be drunk thrice a day for quick relief.
- Drink coconut water as it soothes gastric irritation.
- Take about 5 gms of *elaichi* (cardamom) powder with water and drink it up.
- Take a teaspoon of freshly grated root ginger and add a cup of boiling water to it. Stir for 10 minutes and drink it.  Ginger helps to relax the muscles that line the walls of the oesophagus, so that the stomach acid does not get pushed upwards.
- Practitioners of herbal medicine say that two teaspoons of anise seeds, or caraway, or fennel seeds, added to a cup of boiling water and allowed to mix for 10 minutes before being taken, ease the heartburn.
- Stir a teaspoon of powdered marshmallow root in a cup of water and sip it three or four times a day.

Home Remedies

- Tea made out of crushed cinnamon and boiling water and taken after straining the mixture, cools the heat of the heartburn or acidity.
- Mix half a teaspoon of soda bicarbonate in a few drops of lemon juice added to half a cup of warm water. The lemon juice dispels some of the gas which the soda bicarbonate creates when it comes in contact with hydrochloric acid in the stomach.
- Eat plenty of raw vegetables.
- Better still, extract the juice of vegetables like carrot, cucumber, radish or beetroot and drink it as their alkaline nature counters the effect of acidity.
- Eat smaller and more frequent meals rather than taking heavy breakfast, lunch or dinner.
- Take an anti-acid, like Digene or Mucaine gel for quick relief.
- About 3 gm of Ayurvedic *Avipattikara churan* dissolved in 50 ml. of hot water and taken twice a day for 40 days has a curative effect.

2
Acne

As soon as you enter your teens, your face begins to get pink, white and black pimples. This happens because your skin produces too much sebum — a natural oil lubricant, which blocks your pores. Whipped into action by hormones, which give us sexual maturity, the glands become active but their openings on the skin get clogged.

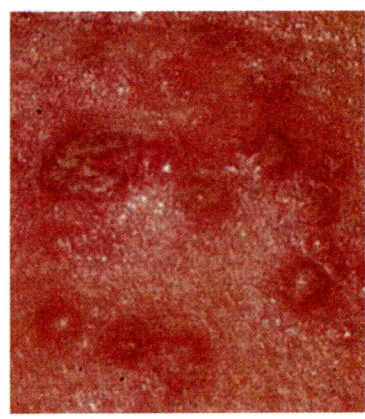

Whiteheads occur and so do pinkish red pimples. When air oxidises the hardened plugs on the skin surface, blackheads raise their head. Young women get these at the time of their periods, while young boys get them by not being careful about cleanliness.

Precautions

- Do not squeeze or pick the spot with a needle or fingers, as it will make things worse.
- Avoid eating oily or fried food.
- Wash your face often with soap and water.
- Wrap an ice cube in a cling film or thin muslin cloth and hold it on to the affected area at least thrice a day. It will reduce the redness of skin.
- Try to keep your bowels working by not allowing constipation to set in.
- Keep your hair clean, as dandruff is a likely cause of acne.

Home Remedies

- Make a paste of turmeric and sandalwood and apply to your face three times a day. Leave the paste on for half an hour and then wash it off with tap water.
- Make a paste out of ground *jeera* (powdered cumin seeds) and apply it over the pimples. Remove the paste after an hour.

- Apply a drop of tea-tree oil to the acne three times a day and leave it on for an hour. It is quite effective in warding off infection, which normally leads to spread of acne.
- To avoid acne cropping up just before the menstrual periods, drink one or two cups of chasteberry tea as it helps to regulate the female hormone.
- *Ajwain* (caraway seeds) made into a paste can be applied any number of times during the day.
- Extract half a cup of juice of aloe vera and drink daily to keep this embarrassing crop of acne away.
- Dip a piece of cottonwood in ginger or lemon juice and leave it on the effected area.
- At times, i.e. when the pimple is just cropping up, application of toothpaste can prevent it from becoming any bigger.
- Add one teaspoon of Epsom salts and three drops of iodine to 125 ml. of water in a pan. Boil it. Let it cool and apply on the face with cotton cool.
- Saturate lettuce leaves in water, apply the pulp to your face and leave for half an hour. Wash off with water.
- Grind bay leaves and blanch in water. Cool and apply on the acne.
- Rub the acne with garlic cloves every day.
- Take *tulsi* (basil) leaves, dissolve in water and make a paste. Apply this paste on the face.
- A paste made out of *jaiphal* (nutmeg) and water is no less effective than *tulsi*.
- *Trifla churan*, available on the counter, can be eaten as it cleans the stomach and prevents acne from erupting.

3

Age Spots

Brown patches on the cheeks, on the top part of arms and feet can be quite a source of embarrassment. What is seen is excessive pigmentation due to years of exposure to hot sunlight. As it takes long to develop, many people do not notice it, but it is always better to nip the disease in the bud. Age spots seem like dark freckles but are normally harmless. If the spots change in size, or become darker in colour, then a dermatologist should be consulted.

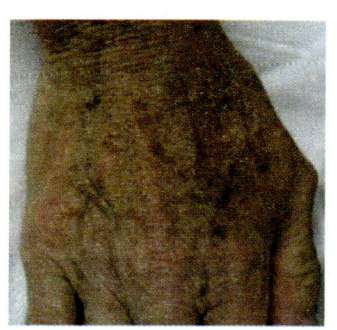

Precautions

- Use a sun cream when going out.
- Use an umbrella to shade yourself from the direct rays of the sun.
- Drink plenty of water and eat fresh fruits to keep the bowels working.

Home Remedies

- Apply lemon juice to the spots at night and go to sleep. It can be applied during the day also and washed off with water after an hour.
- Blanch scented geraniums in boiling water. Strain and cool before applying on the face.
- Blend honey and yoghurt to create a bleaching agent as it helps to lighten the spots. Leave it on for half an hour and wash off.

Home Remedies

- Make a paste out of *neem* leaves or any fruit and honey. Apply on the face and leave for an hour before rinsing your face.
- Apply aloe vera on the brown spots and rub.
- Mix onion juice with ginger (in the proportion of 1:2) and apply on the dark spots.
- Rub a piece of sliced red onion on the age spots. Its juice is acidic enough such that it will help to gradually lighten and fade away the spots.
- If the surface of individual lesions appears rougher than surrounding skin, apply castor oil twice daily with a cotton swab at night.
- Avoid exposure to the sun as far as possible. One who stays in the shade will have much less age spots than one who is exposed to direct sunlight. If one already have age spots, limiting sun exposure will help prevent them from darkening and will minimize recurrence or the appearance of new ones.

4

Alcoholism/Cirrhosis of Liver

This is a chronic ailment in which a person is unable to control consumption of alcohol. Vomiting, disturbed sleep, delirium and illusions are common complaints that alcoholics make. Excessive consumption of alcohol damages the liver, leading to cirrhosis, disorders of the stomach and bowels. At times, the brain cells get damaged or the heart gets weak.

The problem begins with intake of an occasional drink or two before drinking becomes a habit when a person is unable to survive without a drink. For some, alcoholism is a way of socialising while for others it may be a way of escape from the realities of life. Alcoholics slowly acquire a puffy face, bloodshot eyes, a heavy voice and a rapid pulse beat.

In cirrhosis of liver, the normal liver cells are replaced by fibrous scar tissues, which prevent the liver from functioning normally. Once the damage occurs, nothing can repair or replace it. This is accompanied by loss of libido, weight loss, swelling of abdomen, shrinkage of testicles in men and tingling sensation in hands and feet.

Precautions

- Avoid refined foods like sugar, rice, refined flour products and meat.
- Make a firm resolve to break the alcohol habit.
- Resist from smoking.
- Physical exercise should be undertaken religiously.

Home Remedies

- Since grapes contain a pure form of alcohol, alcoholics should take grapes at regular intervals to keep themselves away from liquor.
- A generous consumption of apples curbs intoxication and reduces the craving for alcohol.
- Four to five figs can be dissolved in water and drunk twice daily to gain relief.
- Juice of bitter gourd acts an as antidote to alcohol consumption. Drink three teaspoons of bitter-gourd juice with buttermilk every morning to cure the damaged liver.
- Half a glass of celery juice mixed with an equal amount of water should be taken daily.

- Build up the alcoholic's diet by cleansing his stomach with a generous intake of fruit juice followed by frequent small meals so as to break the drinking habit.
- Take a mixture of lemon juice and mashed onion juice on an empty stomach daily to find relief from cirrhosis.
- The Ayurvedic drugs, called *Yakrut pippali* along with *Arogyavardhini*, prove beneficial in stopping anorexia of liver.

- Take an optimum diet of vital nutrients consisting of wholegrain cereals, nuts, seeds and sprouts, fresh fruits, and vegetables.
- At the beginning of the treatment for alcoholism, in order to relieve the craving as and when it occurs, take a suitable substitute drink for alcohol in form of a glass of fresh fruit juice, or some candy or other snacks as a stimulant.
- All refined foods such as sugar, white rice, macaroni products, strong condiments, white flour, and meat should be avoided.
- If there has been an acute problem of alcoholism, then during his first few days of abstinence, a warm-water enema should be taken everyday to cleanse the bowels. Plenty of rest and outdoor physical exercises are also necessary.

5

Amnesia/Loss of Memory

In amnesia, either partial or complete loss of memory occurs and is most commonly seen among aged persons. Forgetfulness especially regarding names or where you have placed you keys can be highly disconcerting. With age, it becomes difficult to recall facts. Thyroid disorders can affect one's memory besides causing high blood pressure, anxiety and Alzheimer's disease.

The main reason for amnesia to set in is the impairment of brain cells due to poor blood supply caused by circulatory problems.

Home Remedies

- Inhalation of rosemary or basil oil increases the production of beta waves in the brain, creating heightened awareness. Rosemary is an antidote for mental fatigue and forgetfulness.
- People who drink more of coffee suffer less from amnesia than those who drink less of it.
- To increase the flow of blood to the brain, do exercise as it will increase the nerve cells in the brain, preventing illnesses like diabetes and high blood pressure to occur as these contribute to memory lapses.
- An Ayurveda herb, called *Brahmi booti*, dried and ground in water along with seven kernels of almonds, a few peppercorns, and sweetened with sugar, can be taken on an empty stomach.
- Almonds soaked and crushed before eating remove brain debility and cure brain disorders.
- Inhalation of almond oil through the nose every morning and evening is beneficial in fighting brain weakness.

Home Remedies

- Eat reasonably sized meals, fibre-rich whole grains and vegetables rather than white bread, potatoes, rice and pasta.
- Focus on foods like vegetable oils, nuts, seeds, avocados and fish as they maintain the blood sugar levels, preventing closing down of arteries.
- Do regular exercises without fail.
- Drink at least eight glasses of water as dehydration can lead to mental fatigue and amnesia.
- Bananas, chickpeas and turkey are rich in vitamin b and should be eaten with nuts, seeds and wheat grain.

- Avoid foods high in saturated fat.
- Eat fish, two or three times a week.
- Play scrabble, do crossword puzzles, or learn a new language to exercise the brain.
- Consider taking Siberian ginseng, which protects the body against stress and heightens mental activity.
- Figs, walnuts and raisins help to counter brain weakness.
- Apples contain phosphorus and potassium apart from vitamin b that help in synthesis of glutamic acid, that controls the wear and tear of nerve cells.
- Tea prepared with dried sage leaves is found useful in treating loss of memory.
- Cumin seeds mixed with two teaspoons of honey should be taken once a day in the morning.
- Ground black pepper mixed with honey is useful too.
- Phosphorus-rich cow's milk, cereals, pulses, nuts, egg yolk and fruit juices help to control amnesia.
- Adequate sleep and relaxation are conducive to countering loss of memory.

6
Anorexia

The word literally means 'loss of appetite and distaste for food', leading to general weakness. In this illness, people refuse to eat and suffer from insomnia. In course of time, they become emaciated and weak. Today this is a common ailment among young girls who refuse to eat so as to remain slim and trim. It can also occur due to mental problems, emotional disturbances, stress at workplace and general body disorders.

Home Remedies

- Eat one or two oranges daily to activate the flow of digestive juices which aid in digestion and increase the appetite for food.
- Fruits rich in vitamin c are ideal to stimulate the digestive process. *Chapatis* made by kneading wheat dough in grape juice help to improve one's appetite.
- Extract the juice of ginger and lemon and expose it to sunlight for three or four days after adding rock salt to it. A teaspoon of the juice will aid in digestion.
- Apples stimulate the flow of an enzyme called 'pepsin' which invigorates the digestive system.
- Orange juice and water should be take in liberal doses as both are good cleansing agents.
- Use of garlic in vegetables and in soup proves beneficial for a person suffering from anorexia. Garlic can be crushed and licked with a little salt daily.
- Application of an ice-bag over the stomach before meals and take a cool hipbath twice a day to find relief from anorexia.

Home Remedies

- Another remedy is to expose yourself to the sun at 12 o'clock in the afternoon and take a cool air bath the following day by staying out in fresh air. It helps in overcoming anorexia.
- Abdominal massage is also fruitful.
- A warm-water enema will help to eliminate the poisonous toxins from the bowels.
- Ginger is very good to cure loss of appetite. Grind about five grams of ginger and lick it with a little salt once a day.
- It is important to do a thorough cleansing of the digestive tract, for which a 'juice fast' would be helpful. Take the juice of an orange in a glass of warm water, every two hours for three to five days. If orange juice does not agree with the system, only water or half a glass of carrot juice mixed with an equal quantity of water may be taken.
- After the juice fast, adopt an all-fruit diet for some days. Take three meals a day of juicy fruits, such as apples, pears, grapes, grape-fruit, oranges, pineapple, peaches, and melons. Restricted diet of lightly cooked vegetables may be added to the fruit diet.
- Adopt of a sensible diet thereafter, along with a change in the style of living.

7

Appendicitis

Inflammation of the appendix begins with a sudden pain in the centre of the abdomen. Gradually the pain shifts to the lower right side and is accompanied by fever, nausea and vomiting. Excessive amounts of poisonous waste material spreads in the intestinal tract.

Precautions

- Avoid getting constipation as it aggravates the condition of the appendix.

Home Remedies

- Take hot compresses and abdominal packs of wet-sheet strips over the painful area until the acute symptoms subside. Subsequently the patient should be given a warm-water enema till inflammation disappears.
- Eat a well-balanced meal comprising seeds, nuts, grain, vegetables and fruits.
- At the first symptoms of severe pain and vomiting, fasting and a fruit diet should be undertaken.
- An infusion of a tablespoon of green gram taken three times a day is a proven cure for acute appendicitis
- Regular intake of tea made from *methi* (fenugreek) seeds prevents the appendix from accumulating excess mucus and intestinal waste.
- Juice of beet, cucumber and carrot taken twice daily is useful in appendicitis.
- Buttermilk may be taken at regular intervals for treatment of chronic appendicitis.
- Wheat bran and wheat germ can be baked and added to whole wheat before preparing *chapatis* as it prevents the disease.

8

Arteriosclerosis

Thickening of the walls of the arteries is a cause of great concern among old people as fat accumulates in the inner lining of the blood vessel walls. Arteries get narrowed, thus disrupting free circulation of blood.

Signs of inadeqate blood supply generally appear first in the legs with numbness in the feet and cramps in the legs even after a light exercise. lck of physical exercise and a diet rich in cholesterol and refined foods trigger it.

A cerebral vascular stroke with partial, or complete paralysis, of one side of the body, may result if there is blockage with a blood clot. The patient may suffer from high blood pressure, kidney disorders, loss of memory and a confused state of mind.

Precautions

- Avoid smoking.
- Do outdoor physical exercise and avoid mental fatigue.

Home Remedies

- Lemon peel is the richest source of vitamin p that strengthens the arterial system. The peel of one or two lemons may be cut finely, covered with warm water and allowed to stand for 10 hours. A teaspoon of it may be taken before or after every meal.
- Make tea with a teaspoon of dried parsley and warm water. Allow to simmer and take twice or thrice a day.
- Beet juice mixed with carrot and spinach juice is beneficial if taken once a day.

Home Remedies

- Take a glass of water with one teaspoon of honey and lemon juice before going to bed.
- The oil of the herb called *Isabgol* should be taken to prevent and treat arteriosclerosis.
- Garlic and onion have a preventive effect on the development of arteriosclerosis
- A meal of seeds, grain, nuts, vegetables and fruits should be adhered to three times a day.
- Avoid meat, salts and refined or processed foods to control the disease.
- Vegetable oils, particularly sunflower oil, flaxseed oil and olive oil should be the cooking medium.
- When restricting the diet to fruit juice, take a warm-water enema to clear the bowels.
- A prolonged immersion bath at room temperature should be taken before bedtime.
- Squeeze one onion and drink one teaspoon of its juice daily.
- Eat spinach without fail.
- Drink carrot juice to check arteriosclerosis.
- Blanch parsley in a cup of water and drink.

9

Arthritis

This is an inflammation of the joints and is a chronic disease. There are more than 100 types but most common are two types essentially — osteoarthritis, which is a degenerative disease occurring in old age, and the other is rheumatoid which is very serious as it affects the joints of fingers, wrists, hips, knees, as also muscles, tendons and tissues.

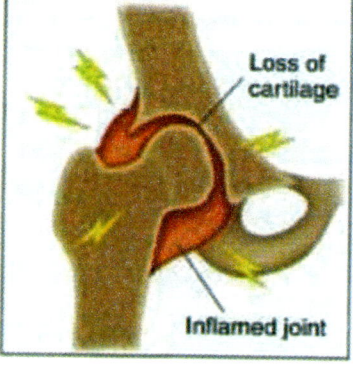
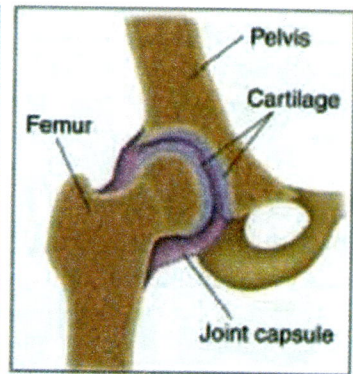

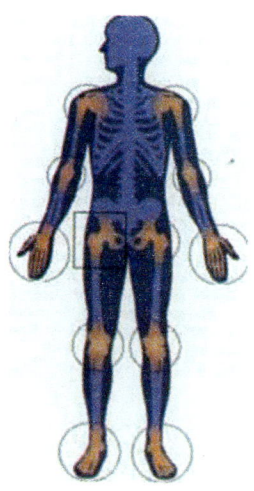

It is said that the patient's inability to produce endorphins or naturally- produced painkillers is a cause. The symptoms include swollen joints due to wear and tear of cartilage. This usually occurs in people above 45 years of age. It is more common among women.

Precautions

- Maintain a normal weight and do not let it increase so as to prevent osteoarthritis of the knees.
- Walk over different kinds of terrain to prevent stress on the same joints every day.
- Do plenty of physical exercise to keep the joints mobile.

Home Remedies

- Take plenty of vitamin C as the antioxidant in it prevents the breakdown of bones by destroying the free radicals. Eat oranges, lemons and other citrus fruits.
- Take 15 mg of zinc every day.
- Take one tablespoon of flaxseed (linseed) oil daily as it contains omega-3. Mix it with orange juice before drinking.
- Massage the affected parts with eucalyptus oil.
- Capsaicin in chillies is a counter-irritant and draws the patient's attention away from the arthritis pain.
- Do yoga exercise as these are ideal, but do them under an expert's guidance.
- Mix 10 gms of dry ginger powder with 15 ml. of castor oil and apply on the joint for relief from painful joints.
- A paste made out of crushed garlic clove and *til* oil (gingely oil) may be applied over the painful joint.
- Heated papaya or castor leaves can be applied over the affected joint.
- Onion juice with warm mustard oil and applied over the painful joint will provide ample relief.
- One of the most successful biological treatments is to place three slices of potatoes without peeling in a glass filled with cold water. The water should be drunk the next morning.
- Raw juice extracted from fresh green leafy vegetables mixed with carrot, celery or red beet is good for arthritis.
- A cup of fresh pineapple juice reduces swelling and inflammation.
- A teaspoon of black sesame seeds soaked in a quarter cup of water at night and taken early next morning prevents frequent joint pain.

Home Remedies

- Drinking water kept in a copper container overnight accumulates traces of copper which strengthens the muscular system.
- Take two teaspoons of calcium lactate in water before meals at least for four months.
- Eating six or eight bananas, a rich source of vitamin B6, proves effective in treating this condition.
- Lime juice diluted in water should be taken every morning as citric acid in lime is a solvent of uric acid, which causes certain types of arthritis.
- Tea made from the herb alfalfa seeds is beneficial.
- Green gram soup mixed with crushed garlic cloves can by taken twice a day.
- Warm coconut or mustard oil with two pieces of camphor and massage on the painful joints. This increases the blood supply and reduces inflammation and stiffness.
- Keep the body warm and do not bandage the painful joint as it restricts the blood circulation.

10 Asthma

Asthma signifies a chronic disorder of the respiratory system in which the air passages in the lungs get narrowed, causing cough, wheezing and shortness of breath. Out of anxiety caused due to difficulty in breathing, an asthma patient seeks prompt action to find relief. What could be the best remedy in such a situation for the patient is to turn to the inhaler. What the patient forgets is that the inhaler is not a cure; it only helps to reduce the symptoms.

Asthma is a commonly occurring disease especially in places, which are dusty, smoky, or abound in pollen, mould or dust mites. At times seven stress, anger or hormonal disturbances can trigger at attack. The spasms or shortness of breath cause coughing and wheezing, followed by release of histamine and other chemicals that cause inflammation and produce mucous. Some patients' pulse rate rises, or causes inability to speak and difficulty in breathing out rather than breathing in. Some patients even complain of attacks of allergy, which is essentially due to the patient being allergic to certain drugs he/she uses.

In an asthmatic patient the bronchi are over-sensitive to allergens or substances present in the air. The state gets aggravated due to emotional stimuli too. The bronchi narrow down making it difficult for air to flow into the lungs. The result is difficulty in breathing with concomitant wheezing (a sound made when breathing out) and need for air. The patient feels a tightness in the chest and an irritating cough may set in. A small amount of mucous or phlegm is released which become black when the condition aggravates.

Precautions

- Guard against pollen, house dust, moulds, pets, especially dogs and cats and pollutants in the air like smoke, etc. and expose the furniture to air and sun. In case of an acute attack consult a doctor and use bronchodilators to free the blocked bronchi.

Home Remedies

- First and foremost try to stay calm during an attack. Getting into a flap will not help in any case. Take deep breaths and feel your lungs expand and fill with fresh air. Repeat this exercise a number of times till some relief is felt.
- Put half a teaspoon of licorice root tea in a cup of hot water and let it stand for 10 minutes. Pass this through a strainer and drink.
- Drink a cup of coffee or a Cola drink as both are rich in caffeine, a chemical related to theophylline — a drug used in asthma. It immediately opens the air passages in the lungs.
- Mix juice of one clove of garlic (peeled) with one teaspoon of honey and take twice a day. It will dilate the bronchial tubes. However this remedy is not suitable for patients with ulcers or bleeding disorders.
- Blend radish, honey and lemon juice in a blender for 20 minutes. Pour this mixture into a pan and cook on low heat. Take one teaspoon daily.
- Sit in a place where the air is cool and relax, taking deep breaths. Avoid thinking of things that cause worry or tension.
- Mix half a teaspoon of *hing* (asafoetida), 50 mls. of sesame oil and a pinch of camphor. Apply this on the chest to find relief from congestion and uneasiness.
- A glass of milk helps to cool you down.
- Fresh cabbage juice taken daily proves effective to some extent.
- Oily fish such as tuna, salmon and mackerel is an effective as a glass of asthma drugs that are called leukotriene inhibitors. These drugs stop the action of compounds that cause inflammation in the airways. Better still would be to take six capsules of 100 mg fish oil daily in divided doses.
- *Haldi* (turmeric), that is used to flavour all our cuisine, is a powerful anti-inflammatory. Take one teaspoon of turmeric powder in a cup of warm milk and drink it three times a day. Certain health-food stores even stack turmeric capsules to make our work easier.
- Coloured fruits and vegetables have a powerful anti-inflammatory and anti-allergic action. Take 500 mg of quercetin three times a day, some 20 minutes before taking your meals.
- Drink two tablespoon of fresh lemon juice in one tablespoon of water.
- Boil fresh cranberries in water and mash them. Take this two to three times daily.

Home Remedies

- Drink a cup of hot dark tea, preferably using the Lipton teabags.
- Mix one teaspoon of green ginger juice, betel leaf juice of one clove of garlic. Take one teaspoon three times a day.
- Permanent relief is provided by *gur* (jaggery) mixed with equal quantity of mustard oil continuously for 21 days.
- Boil one teaspoon of pure honey with one teaspoon of olive oil and half a cup of water. Drink it daily.
- Blanch and drink wild cherry tree bark.
- Make pills of pea size with *kapur* (camphor) and *hing* (asafoetida) and take one or two pills with hot water three to four times daily.
- Mix the powder of *pipal* with *sendha namak* (rock salt) and ginger juice to drink regularly for a week.
- Mix juice of *tulsi* (basil) leaves in honey and take three times a day.
- Put fennel oil in a burner and breathe in the fumes.
- Close your bathroom and fill it with hot water. Breathe in the steam. Otherwise boil water in a pot. Remove from the fire and lean towards the pot to inhale the steam after covering the pot and your face with a towel.
- Crush papal, *amla* (Indian gooseberry) and *sonth* in a stone grinder and take with honey, *mishri* (sugar candy) and *ghee* (clarified butter) to ward of mild attacks.
- In the Ayurveda system of medicine, *Sitopaladi churan* mixed with two teaspoon of honey is taken. Better still is to take 5-10 gms of *Chavanprasha* with milk before going to bed.

11

Athlete's Foot

Our feet facilitate our movements, allowing us to stand, walk, run, jump and dance. We just cannot do without them. The feet however, tend to suffer from an ailment called 'athlete's foot'. Caused by a fungus called *Tinea pedis*, the irritating infection derives its name because it essentially attacks the area between the toes, causing itching and flaking of the affected area. It may also target the toenails, skin, hair and the soles and sides of the feet, causing oozing blisters in more severe cases.

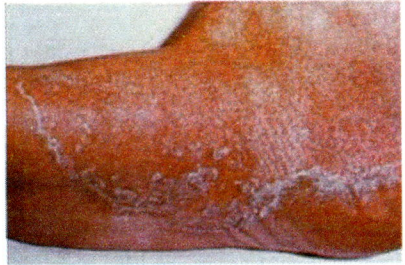

The disease is caused by walking barefoot on damp floors, like that of the bathroom or on the edges of the swimming pool. The fungus is so infectious that it may not even spare your sweaty and rain-soaked socks and shoes.

Precautions

- Keep your feet dry as far as possible and if they do get wet, then dry with a towel and sprinkle talcum powder between the toes of the feet.
- Wash your hands thoroughly after removing your socks and shoes.
- Wear your underwear or trousers/skirt after wearing the socks so that the fungus does not spread from your toes.
- If, not treated on time, the skin may crack, allowing bacteria to penetrate into the skin.
- Try wearing cotton socks and undergarments even if they are more expensive than the synthetic ones.
- Change into a fresh pair of socks every day. Avoid wearing the already worn socks.
- Wash socks in very hot water to kill the germs.

Precautions

- Instead of roaming around barefoot, wear loose slippers when entering the bathroom or near the swimming pool.
- Yellow, brittle and thick toenails mean fungal infection, which may lead to athlete's foot. Cut the toenails, but avoid clipping of the edges, else you might face in-growing toenails.

Home Remedies

- Make a paste of one tablespoon of soda bicarbonate by adding water. Rub in the paste over the infected area. Leave for an hour before washing off and drying your feet. Dust cornflower on top.
- As tea contains tannic acid, which is an astringent, add one teaspoon of tea to boiling water for five minutes in half a tub. Cool it till the water is lukewarm and tolerable for the feet to be soaked in it. Leave for half an hour before drying the feet thoroughly well.
- Add two teaspoons of salt to half a tub of warm water. Immerse your feet in it for five to 10 minutes. Remove your feet and again dip in the water. Repeat this two to three times every day.
- Apply surgical spirit three or four times a day.
- If not the above, then try vinegar or hair spray for obtaining relief.
- The micro-organisms in yoghurt/curd prove beneficial if rubbed on the infected area. Let it dry for some time and then wash off the curd.
- Add a few drops of mustard oil to warm water in a tub and soak your feet in it for half an hour. Dry the feet after taking your feet out of the water.
- Herbal remedy also helps, for instance, rub calendula ointment or lavender oil on the feet.
- Tea-tree oil mixed with olive oil or lavender by taking two to three drops of each and rubbed over the affected foot prove beneficial.

12

Backache

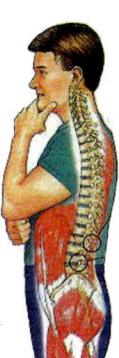

Once a spasm or ache is experienced in the back, the problem continues to occur every now and then. Normally bad posture is responsible for backache or it is due to weak muscles and development of flab. The back is not able to bear the extra weight and gives way. Prolonged sitting, standing or stooping in one position causes the back to pain. Sudden vigorous jerking or twisting of the back causes it to pain. For immediate relief, doctors prescribe cold compress for two to three days followed by application of heat or infra-red rays from an infra-red lamp. This has to he followed by stretching and strengthening exercises for a month or two, to put the back into action.

In modern life, time and stress put pressure on the nerves and since the spinal column, from the base of the head till the lumbar region, has to wear the brunt of it, it suffers the maximum.

Home Remedies

- Apply ice to relieve pain as it temporarily reduces the swelling. Even frozen peas can serve the same purpose.
- After about two days, switch over to moist heat to stimulate the blow flow and reduce the spasms. Dip a towel in very warm water, fold it and place it on the painful area of the back, after lying on bed on your stomach.
- Buy a heating pad and leave it on your back for 20 minutes every day, till relief is achieved.
- Ask someone to massage the back.
- Take a warm bath and sit in the tub for some time.
- Put buckwheat on a warm cloth and apply on the back.

Home Remedies

- If the pain is in the lower back, then rock the pelvis from side to side and front to back.
- Go for a swim or do stretching exercises.
- Eat nuts, particularly almonds and walnuts daily.
- Rub your back with mint oil or almond oil.
- In case of prolonged standing in one position, keep one foot on a platform or stool.
- If the back of your chair gives poor support, place a cushion behind, in the hollow of your back.
- Sleep on a firm mattress.
- Avoid sleeping face down.
- Keep one knee bent when lying on one side.
- Rest in bed to allow the injured muscles to heal
- Take a tablespoon of *sonth,* soda bicarbonate and salt with hot, mild or lukewarm water.
- In olden days, a mustard poultice was a favourite remedy for backache. As mustard is warm, it gives a tingling sensation that distracts attention from the deeper pain. The poultice in made by taking one part of powdered mustard with two parts of flour and adding water to make a paste. Spread it on an old towel and apply it like a compress on the aching part. Protect the skin by rubbing petroleum jelly before using the poultice.
- At times, you get sciatica, i.e. pain in the roots of the sciatic nerve lying near the base of the spine, then the sciatic roots are under pressure from a herniated disc. A sensation of numbness extends down the legs to your feet and toes. In this case apply the poultice of mustard powder on the lower back and rest.

13

Bad Breath

When your gums, tongue and teeth harbour odour-causing bacteria, bad breath is caused. In the olden days, *paan* (betel leaf) was used as a *mukhshodhak* (mouth freshener). Bad breath can be due to pungent foods, inflamed sinuses, respiratory infections or digestive problems. Further, it can also be due to consumption of any dish laced with onion, garlic, blue cheese or pepperoni. A chronically dry mouth or too many cups of coffee can even cause bad breath.

Bad breath is also due to pyorrhea, which is characterised by copious discharge of pus from the root of the teeth and gums.

Precautions

- Avoid the garlic family in vegetables.
- Avoid fish, especially the uncooked fish.
- Do not skip meals as it causes foul breath due to reduction in the production of saliva, which keeps the teeth, tongue and gums clean.
- Use a toothbrush to clean the teeth thoroughly well.
- Rinse your mouth very often with clean water.
- Keep your tongue clean.
- Plain indigestion or an ulcer can cause bad breath.
- At times, physiological processes like menstrual periods, egg release or pregnancy can cause bad breath due to hormonal changes.

Home Remedies

- Certain herbs and spices like *laung* (cloves), *saunf* (aniseeds), or *elaichi* (cardamoms) cover foul smell of your breath.
- If you have pyorrhoea, brush your teeth with the prop-root of banyan.
- Twigs of *neem* can be used for brushing teeth.
- *Triphala* powder is useful to rid oneself of constipation which causes bad smell.
- Vegetables like *karela* (bitter gourd), potato and drumstick are useful in keeping off bad smell.
- Chew peppermint to fight bad breath.
- Swallow one tablespoon of apple cider vinegar before each meal.
- Eat pumpkin regularly to fight bad breath.
- Brush your teeth with baking soda.
- Blanch parsley and drink it several times.
- Drink camomile tea.
- Blanch thyme-leaved savoury and gargle with it.
- Gargle with salty water.
- Chew peppermints, chewing gums or lozenges to keep bad breath at bay.
- Get an orange peel and eat it. The citric acid in the peel encourages the flow of breath-freshening saliva.
- Chew on fennel, dill, cardamom and anise seeds, as they kill the bacteria on the tongue.
- Suck a stick of cinnamon as a mouth antiseptic.

14

Bites/Stings

People living near the equator or in dusty and swampy places have to confront mosquitoes, bees and wasps. It is necessary to prevent an assault from these irritating predators and protect your skin. Some insects bite when they are hungry and in search of food. A bite leaves a maddeningly ugly bump, while bees and wasps penetrate the skin that pains maddeningly.

Home Remedies

- On being stung, soak the area affected in vinegar, or in a solution of soda bicarbonate in water. For bee stings, use an alkaline neutraliser, and for wasp stings, which are alkaline, use acidic vinegar to neutralise.
- Crush one or two aspirin tablets on a chopping board and add water to make a paste. Dab this on the sting and the aspirin will neutralise the venom.
- Rub the graphite end of a matchstick on the bee- or wasp-sting.
- Cut a tomato in half and apply the inner side with the seeds on the sting for a few minutes.
- Apply aloe vera followed by lavender on the sting.
- A wet mud applied on the sting helps.
- Apply an ice pack to numb the area and suppress the swelling. Tie ice cubes in a towel and leave the ice pack on the affected area.
- The enzymes found in papaya neutralise the insect venom.
- Make a thin paste of sugar and water to apply on the sting.
- Rub a slice of crushed onion or garlic over the sting because the enzymes in these vegetables neutralise the effect of the sting.

Home Remedies

- Apply baking soda on the sting.
- Smear egg-yolk on the sting to find relief from pain.
- The swelling of the bite can be reduced by applying a drop of tea-tree oil on the area several times during the day.
- To prevent itching due to insect bite, dab a drop or two of lavender oil on the sting.
- Calendula cream can be rubbed in many times during the day.
- Dip a piece of cotton wool in eucalyptus oil, clove oil, or peppermint oil and place on the sting. It will stop the itching that the sting causes.
- Since toothpastes contain peppermint, apply any one on the sting.
- Underarm deodorants can be sprayed on the sting as they reduce the irritation on the skin.
- An anti-itch spray or gel that contains menthol acts as a good skin-soother.
- Citronella, a lemony scented oil, repels insects.

15
Body Odour

When sweat accumulates in any part of the body, it emits body odour which can be very unpleasant and affects your social life. Stress, ovulation, sexual excitement, fear and anger can lead to excessive sweating and body odour. The apocrine glands in the armpit and groins secrete a substance that attracts bacteria and cause strong odour. Nervousness, or anxiety, or heavy exercise, must prepare you for developing unpleasant odour.

If you drink alcohol, smoke cigarettes or cigar, you can emit a strong odour. Poor hygiene is essentially the main cause for body odour. Too much sweating can be due to an overactive thyroid gland, low blood sugar or problem with the nervous system.

Home Remedies

- Shave regularly under your arms to stop bacteria from forming and causing body odour.
- Wear fresh clothes everyday. Never wear yesterday's clothes. However clean your body is, the clothes will retain the smell of yesterday's sweat. Apply tea-tree oil as it kills bacteria.
- Wash clothes thoroughly, particularly clothing that comes into contact with sweaty areas such as socks, underwear and shirts
- Essential oils of lavender, lime and peppermint fight bacteria which cause bad smell.
- The herb sage can reduce perspiration.
- Soak yourself in water with tomato juice in it for 15 minutes.
- As certain foods cause excessive sweat, avoid sugar, white flour, hydrogeneted oils and processed foods. Keep away from alcohol, cumin, garlic and caffeine.

Home Remedies

- Prepare a solution of vinegar, salt and baking powder and keep it in a spray bottle. Apply it after a bath. It will prevent odour for at least eight to 10 hours a day.
- Eat nuts, sprouts and fresh fruits.
- Take a thorough bath every day. Use a good soap while bathing. Clean yourself properly, particularly your armpits, groin and feet which produce a lot of sweat..
- Some people have more sweat and oil producing glands than others. If you sweat a lot, you may need to shower / bathe two or three times a day.
- Eat plenty of spinach and leafy green vegetables.
- Chew a few sprigs of parsley.
- Lime-tree tea stimulates the excretion of waste products from the body.

16 Boils

Sometimes a pimple on the skin becomes big and forms an abscess or a furuncle. Bacteria work their way down the hair follicles into your skin. The boil fills with pus and swells. Usually a boil bursts on its own in about two weeks or due to rubbing of clothing over it.

Boils are quite painful, especially in areas where the skin is attached to the underlying tissue, such as in the nose, ears or fingers. The common sites for boils are the face, neck, buttocks and thighs.

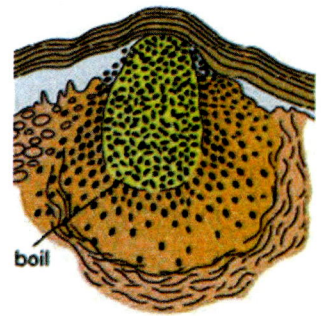

Boils generally appear when a person is in a rundown and weak condition.

Home Remedies

- Apply egg yolk over the boil and it will burst to start the healing process.
- Juice of onion or garlic may be applied on the boils to ripen them, break apart and ooze out pus.
- A cupful of fresh juice of bitter gourd mixed with lime juice should be sipped on an empty stomach daily.
- Make a poultice with one teaspoon of milk cream, half a teaspoon of vinegar and a pinch of turmeric powder. It helps in ripening the boil.
- Warm a betel leaf till it is soft. Coat it with castor oil and place the leaf over the inflamed part. Replace with a new leaf till the boil ruptures.
- Grind cumin seeds in water to make a paste to apply on the boils.
- Extract juice of barley and wrap it in muslin before applying on the boil.

Home Remedies

- Roast turmeric powder and apply over the boil to make it burst or ripen.
- Warm compresses may be applied often.
- Avoid constipation.
- A warm, moist tea bag will act as a compress.
- Make a compress with thyme or camomile tea to prevent spread of infection.
- Dust on some talc to reduce moisture and perspiration formation, especially where the skin hurts.
- Use a liquid anti-bacterial soap to clean the boil and the surrounding skin.
- Apply tomato paste on and around the boil. Cover this with a piece of gauze and tape and leave it on overnight. The next morning the boil would have burst or would be about to burst.
- Mix some flour with a few drops of vinegar. Make it a thick paste . Apply this paste to the boil and cover with gauze or a bandaid. Leave this overnight. The next morning the paste would have hardened. Much like a cast. when you pull this off the head will come out with it allowing the pus to ooz.

17

Bronchitis

Bronchitis is caused due to inflammation of the bronchial tubes within the lungs, resulting in discharge of phlegm or sputum. It is caused due to viral infection when the bronchi swell, mucus accumulates, forcing you to cough forcefully. It may be accompanied by aches, shortness of breath, fatigue, chills, cough and raised temperature. Pain in the chest and loss of appetite may also accompany the above symptoms.

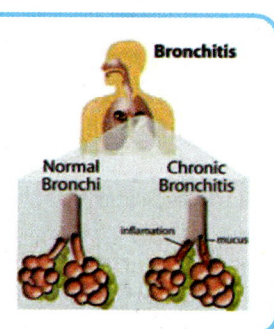

Precautions

- Stop smoking with immediate effect.
- Avoid curd and sour food.
- Banana and guava should not be taken as they facilitate mucous formation.
- Keep yourself warm and away from exposure to cold winds and rain.
- Avoid smoking in dusty or stuffy atmosphere.

Home Remedies

- Eat hot spicy food like salsa, or chilli pepper, or cayenne pepper, as these will help you to cough out the phlegm accumulated inside.
- Take a garlic clove with water on an empty stomach.
- Prepare a decoction of basil leaves, mint leaves, cloves and black pepper and take two or three times a day.

Home Remedies

- Add half a teaspoon of turmeric powder to a glass of milk and drink two times daily on an empty stomach.
- Take half a teaspoon each of the powders of ginger, pepper and cloves thrice daily.
- Drink one teaspoon of onion juice every morning as it has expectorant properties.
- Mix spinach leaves, water and a pinch of ammonium chloride with honey and drink.
- Mix sesame seeds, linseed, common salt, and honey and take once at night.
- A similar type of emulsion can be prepared with almond kernels and orange or lemon juice.
- Take a teaspoon of honey and powdered herb called 'chicory' as it is beneficial.
- A hot poultice of *alsi* (linseed) made in water can be applied on the chest and the back.
- Take a hot Epsom-salt bath at night.
- Apply a towel soaked in hot water over the upper chest.
- Inhale steam by boiling water and putting a drop or two of eucalyptus or pine oil in it.
- Take vitamin C or vitamin C-rich food daily.
- Boil a cup of water, remove from fire and add two teaspoons of mullein flowers in it. Strain and drink three cups a day.
- In an acute attack of bronchitis, drink thyme tea.

18 Bruises

A bruise is a hurt, or scratch, or superficial hurt, which is tender, painful to touch and reddish in colour. After a day or two, it turns purple and while healing, it is yellow or grey in colour. It heals finally without fear of infection setting in as the skin is not broken or exposed to air. It is caused when you receive a bump, a blow or a knock to damage the small vessels in your skin.

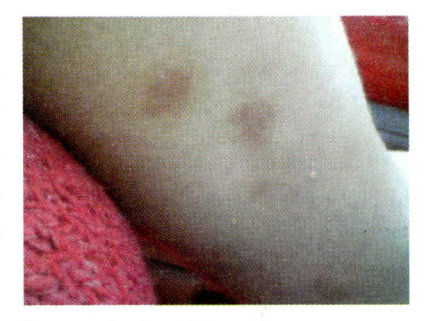

It may cause pain due to minor tears in blood vessels underneath the skin.

Home Remedies

- Apply an ice-pack on the bruise to reduce inflammation. A day later, apply a heating pad to the affected area to dilate the blood vessels.
- Apply apple cider vinegar and cold water on the bruise.
- Apply *arnica* herb or gel on the bruise.
- Crush fresh parsley leaves and spread them over the bruise.
- Vinegar mixed with warm water and applied on the bruise helps.
- Eat plenty of carrots, apricots and citrus fruits as they contain flavonoids which help in the healing process.
- Steep mullein flowers in olive oil and apply on the bruise.
- Break a raw egg and apply on the bruise.
- Apply comfrey or buchu tea on the bruise to reduce pain.
- Apply witch hazel on the bruise.

19

Burns

Dry or wet heat can cause scalding or burning of skin. Burns cause serious injury to body tissues and it can be either due to heat or chemicals or radiation. As burns affect the skin first, there is danger of infection as the skin gets damaged, allowing the germs to enter inside.

Worst cases of burn take place at home when you burn your fingers in the fire, or drop scalding water on your feet, or hot oil or grease drops fly on to your face when deep frying anything.

The mildest form of burn, called first degree', causes redness with swelling. More serious injuries can be due to fire, steam or chemicals (second degree) in which blisters form and cause pain. The third degree burns are those where the skin gets charred or scalded, turning black, white or red. There is no pain but swelling is immense and thus calls for hospitalisation as the patient is in a state of shock.

Precautions

- Stay away from hot drinks.
- Avoid hot spicy food.

Home Remedies

- If only the top layer of the skin its affected, then put the burnt area under cold running water for at least half an hour. Use cold milk or ice only if water is short.
- After the initial cold water treatment, wet cloth can be placed on the burn.

Home Remedies

- Ensure that if the blisters form in 'third degree' or 'second degree' burns, do not let them break.
- The modern theory is to let the burn or any open wound open to air and not cover it up as healing is faster when the wound is exposed.
- Squeeze fresh aloe vera gel from the plant and apply to the burn to reduce pain and keep bacteria at bay.
- Fine turmeric powder can be applied with some honey.
- Make a paste out of dry coconut and coconut oil and apply over the burn.
- Soak a cotton cloth in a strong infusion of camomile and apply to the burn.
- Soak flannel in ice-cold whole milk and apply to the burn.
- The Indian pennywort or *gotu kola* has valuable healing properties and is available as a capsule as also an ointment to heal burns.
- If the mouth is scalded, then gargle with salt water or suck ice cubes.
- Calendula ointment made from marigolds can be applied as often as possible.
- Hypericum ointment contains hypericin, which heals the burnt area.
- Juice extracted from the stem of plantain tree can be applied.
- A paste made of an egg, the powder of gum of the *babul* tree and coconut oil makes a good medicine.
- If only a burning sensation is felt, then make a poultice of *mehndi* (henna) leaves and vinegar or lemon juice and apply on the burn for relief.
- An ointment prepared with pure *ghee* (clarified butter), *raal* and white *jeera* (cumin seeds) is a good healer.

Cervical Spondylosis

Age brings with it a number of related diseases. Severe pain in the neck region is one, and is caused due to arthritis affecting the inter-vertebral discs of the spine. It is called 'cervical spondylosis'. Trauma, incorrect posture, sedentary lifestyle or writing with head bent for long, aggravate the problem.

The pain at times is so severe that it spreads to the shoulders, arms and chest. Even the forehead may get affected. Giddiness or numbness of fingers may follow; it is then that a doctor or physiotherapist may have to be called to help.

Precautions

- Avoid refined flour and semolina. Eat wheat with husk.
- Keep away from the cold.
- Desist from eating curd, tamarind and other sour items.

Home Remedies

- *Neem* is ideal in spondylosis. The flowers and leaves can be made into a paste and taken daily.
- Any oil, like coconut or olive, can be mixed with camphor and used for massage. It has the same effect as Relaxyl or Moov ointment has.
- Take a clove of garlic daily on an empty stomach.

21

Chickenpox

Caused by *Varicella zoster* virus, chickenpox makes its appearance as a rash or red spots beginning on the trunk, before spreading all over the body. There can be a few spots or hundreds of them. Over 10 days, the spots may turn into small blisters, which break. Slowly scabs form and gradually fall off. It affects mostly young children.

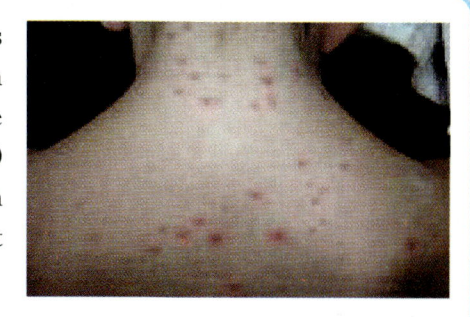

The symptoms appear after a week of catching the infection. A running nose and sore eyes are the early symptoms.

Chickenpox is accompanied by fever and headache, severe pain in the limbs and cough. A person may vomit out. It is infectious and prevent other children from going near the patient.

Precautions

- Prevent the child from going out in the sun.
- Once the attack is over, apply a sunscreen before the child leaves home.
- Let the child wear thin, soft clothes.

Home Remedies

- Give cold drinks and cold ice cream made of water and essence to keep the child's insides clean.

Home Remedies

- Give cold baths to the child when the spots itch, which is usually when scales form.
- Give the child a bath in soda bicarbonate mixed in water which is lukewarm.
- If the child has chickenpox in the mouth, then give salt water to gargle.
- Keep fresh *neem* leaves under the pillow of the child.
- Make a mixture of turmeric powder and *tulsi* (basil) leaves by boiling and cooking it. Make the child drink it a few times per day.
- If the child has cough, then the juice of basil leaves is mixed with honey and given.
- Though some people apply a paste of *neem* leaves and sandalwood, it is better not to do so as the blisters may burst.
- Keep the child cool in a well-ventilated room.

22

Common Cold/Flu

Doctors and medical scientists have been knocking their brains off to discover a cure for cold but it is nowhere in sight. It begins with a sniffle, goes on to sneezing, coughing, and at times, develops into a fever (102°F), accompanied with headache, muscle ache, fatigue and nausea to become flu. Though called a mild sickness, it lasts for a week or 10 days, leaving you very weak, enervated and down-in-the-dumps for days afterwards.

Studies reveal that the external cold climate leaves us open to viruses that infect the upper respiratory tract, affecting the nose and the throat. It is more common among the young as their system is unable to fight the hundreds of different viruses that cause the cold. As we grow older, our immune system becomes stronger and we get fewer colds.

Precautions

- During the winter months, keep yourself well protected by wearing warm clothes.
- Since a cold is very contagious, keep yourself protected by drinking the juice of citrus fruits, lemon, oranges or popping in a pill of vitamin c.
- Blow one nostril at a time, else the reverse pressure can send the virus into your nose.
- Try not to touch a doorknob, a telephone, or other objects used by a person afflicted with cold.
- Curd, cold water and cold drinks should be avoided.

Home Remedies

- To 120 ml. of water, add a quarter teaspoon of salt and boil. Put two or three drops of this saline in your nose five or six times a day.

Home Remedies

- Relax and do not over-exert.
- Drink plenty of fluids as a runny nose leads to loss of water, thus draining your water reserves.
- Drink hot beverages and clear soups to feel better.
- Eat a balanced diet that contains plenty of fresh fruits and vegetables.
- Gargle with tea-water or saline water warmed slightly.
- Inhale steam through a covered pan of boiling water or a teakettle containing boiling water. While inhaling, cover your face with one end of the towel and the kettle with the other end.
- Prepare black tea with black pepper, dry ginger and *tulsi* (basil) leaves. Drink this tea three to four times a day to get relief from a runny nose or a sore throat.
- Add half a teaspoon of turmeric powder to a cup of hot milk and drink thrice a day. Ginger can be added if desired.
- Grate root ginger or horse-radish and eat a small amount to clear out congestion.
- Add one tablespoon of mustard powder to a litre of hot water in a large tub. Soak your feet in this tub. The mustard draws blood to your feet, helping you find relief from congestion.
- Make a poultice with three tablespoons of mustard powder added to a cup of flour or fine oatmeal and warm water. First spread a layer of petroleum jelly on your chest to protect against the warm water. Slap on the poultice over the area lined with petroleum jelly. Do not leave the poultice for more than 15 minutes. The pungent smell of mustard clears the blocked sinuses and improves blood circulation.
- Add a few drops of eucalyptus oil to your handkerchief and smell it whenever the nose gets congested. Inhaling it will clear the nose.
- To make a steam inhalation, add a few drops of thyme or eucalyptus oil to warm water. Inhale the steam but keep your eyes closed as the oil can irritate your eyes.
- Practise relaxation techniques because the more stressed you are, the more prone you are to a cold.

23 Conjunctivitis

When the eyes become red, itch and ooze out a secretion, it means inflammation of the conjunctiva — a transparent membrane that covers the 'sclera' or white of the eye. This inflammation is known as conjunctivitis. Commonly known as 'pink eye', it can be due to bacterial or viral infection or an allergic reaction to contact lens, cosmetics or pollen. The sticky discharge glues your eyelashes and eyelids when you are asleep.

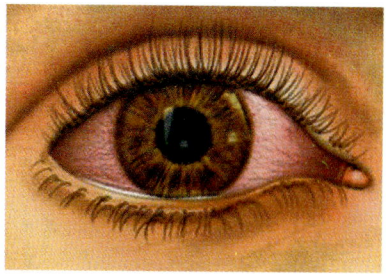

Symptoms

- redness in the eye
- a burning sensation
- sensitivity to light
- dryness
- grittiness sensation
- pain
- itchy, scratchy feeling
- watering of the eyes
- sometimes a sticky discharge that may cause eyelashes and eyelids to become stuck together while you are asleep

Precautions

- Wear dark glasses when going out.
- Keep a handkerchief ready to wipe the discharge from the eyes.
- Keep your clothes, towels, cosmetics separately from others.

Home Remedies

- Soak a piece of cloth or flannel in warm water and use it as a compress. Then soak another piece of cloth in ice-cold water and place on the eyes. Repeat the process five or six times a day to find relief.
- Boil water and add a teaspoon of salt to it to simmer for 15 minutes and cool. Use an eyedropper and squeeze a few drops in your eyes.
- Fresh breast milk is the best remedy for conjunctivitis. Put a few drops five times daily.
- Take the Ayurvedic *Triphala churan*, soak in a glass of water for half an hour and boil till it is half its content. Filter it through a muslin cloth and wash your eyes with the clear water three or four times.
- Boil camomile tea in warm water and cool. Soak a cloth in it and keep over your eyes.
- Beat in a blender a few coriander leaves with water. Strain the juice and apply on the closed eyelids for a few minutes. Wipe the juice and open your eyes.
- Steep a teaspoon of coriander seeds in boiling water for 15 minutes, strain and cool it. Wash your eyes in it by keeping the eyes closed.
- Consult a doctor if the case is severe and he will advise you to take an oral antihistamine to relieve the itching.

24

Constipation

Constipation is caused due to improper functioning of the bowels and this happens due to a lack of dietary fibre or water in the diet. Constipation may also be due to lack of exercise, or hypothyroidism, diabetes, depression, or irritable bowel syndrome.

Precautions

- If you do not respond to nature's call, then withholding of stool may lead to constipation.
- Do not force yourself to clear the bowels, as exertion of undue pressure may cause piles or anal fissures.

Home Remedies

- Take long morning walks as they help you to move food through your bowel.
- Take a laxative, like a hot cup of milk, as it may stimulate the colon.
- Lemon juice is a good laxative.
- Dandelion tea has a mild laxative effect.
- Mix one or two teaspoons of crushed *Isabgol* (psyllium) seeds in a cup of hot water and drink.
- Flaxseeds are high in fibre and good for stimulating digestion.
- Eat more *rotis* (bread) of wheat or *jowar* (maize).
- Take plenty of green vegetables and fibrous fruits.
- Avoid excessive tea and coffee.
- Cut down on smoking/drinking.

Home Remedies

- Take dried prunes or chew raisins.
- Take senna as a natural laxative.
- Eat bran cereals, whole meal bread, baked beans, figs, kidney beans, peanuts, dates, apples, pears, porridge and sprouts.
- Half of a medium-sized papaya should be eaten at breakfast as it acts like a laxative.
- Raw spinach juice mixed with water should be taken twice daily.

25 Corns

Corns and calluses are areas of thickened skin that arise due to constant pressure or friction. The corns are smaller than calluses and arise on the toes whereas calluses develop on the soles of the feet. A corn is usually painful. Corns are shaped like pyramids with the apex pointing inwards. They are tender to the touch. At times, warts on the feet are mistaken for corns. Corns usually occur due to improper footwear.

Calluses on the hands and feet are painless but if it presses on a bone or nerve, then it can be painful and a constant source of irritation.

Precautions

- Wear shoes and sandals that fit the feet properly — neither too tight nor too loose.
- If you are diabetic, then a callus or corn on the foot is dangerous as it is at high risk of contacting infection.
- Keep your feet clean and dry.
- Wear high heels only on certain occasions.

Home Remedies

- Make a paste by grinding three or four liquorice sticks and mixing them with a teaspoon of sesame oil or mustard oil. This should be rubbed into the hardened skin at bedtime. Gradually the skin will soften and the corn decreases in size.
- A fresh slice of lemon should be tied over the painful corn at night and allowed to stay for the night.

Home Remedies

- Half a teaspoon of raw papaya juice may be applied thrice daily.
- Some people file corns and calluses with a callus file but it can be painful.
- Rub olive oil on the corn to soften it daily. Cover it up with a corn protector or pad. Else apply a few drops of castor oil to the corn with a cotton bud and secure with adhesive tape over the pad to hold it in place.
- Soak the foot with the corn in water containing Epsom salts.
- Apply the corn-removing patches that contain salicylic acid after a bath. The acid causes burning of the hard skin.
- Crush five aspirin tablets and mix in half a teaspoon of lemon juice and half a teaspoon of water. Dab the paste on to the thickened skin, wrap the foot with cling film and cover with a heated towel. Remove the wrap after 10 minutes and generally scrub the loosened skin with pumice stone.
- Soak your feet in a bowl of warm water every week and then apply a moisturising lotion.
- A bulb of Indian squill is roasted and applied over the corn. Tie a bandage over it at night.
- The milky juice of green figs can be applied twice or thrice daily to soften corns.
- Grind a small piece of chalk and apply over the corn.
- Apply a slice of pineapple and tie it over the corn every night. The corn will cure after a few weeks.
- Make a paste of washing soda and lime by using water. Apply this over the corn at night. Repeat for a few nights till the skin dries and sheds off.
- Turmeric powder mixed in honey or *neem* oil should be applied on the corn.
- A gentle application of coconut or castor oil on the corn three to four times daily softens it.

26

Cough/Sore Throat

A sore throat, which later develops into cough, is a common illness during the winter months. It begins as an infection of the upper respiratory tract, causing inflammation of the trachea or windpipe. In a bad case of cough, mucus accumulates which one spits out as phlegm. This is normally caused due to an allergy. A dry cough is usually caused through inhalation of cigarette smoke or dust or pollen grains, making you hack on and off.

Most coughs are 'good' for the lungs, so it is advisable to allow it to take its normal course of 10 days. If during coughing, blood comes out and is accompanied by bacteria and chest pain, a doctor should be consulted immediately.

If it is barking cough, caused by a viral or bacterial infection, it is called 'croup'. If it is whooping cough, which affects children of one- to five-years old, and is caused by bacteria invading the nasal passage, respiratory tract and lungs, leading to violent bouts of cough, then a physician needs to be consulted.

Home Remedies

- Any cough drop or boiled sweets or lozenges made from the bark of the slippery elm tree are helpful.
- Use a double boiler or place a bowl containing four tablespoons of honey and six chopped onions in a bowl and keep it over a pan of boiling water. Cover and cook for two hours. Strain and take one or two tablespoons of this mixture after every two hours.
- Mix 20 gms of turmeric powder in a cup of warm milk. Drink this twice a day till 15 days.
- Mix 5mls. of *tulsi* (basil) leaves, 10 ml. of pure honey and chew this ball twice a day till the cough is cured.

Home Remedies

- Mix two tablespoons of lemon juice, a tablespoon of honey and a pinch of cayenne powder. If cayenne is not available, use freshly grated onion. The lemon juice provides the infection-fighting vitamin C, the honey soothes the throat, cayenne hastens the healing process while onion triggers the cough reflex, making you throw out phlegm.
- Mix five or six cloves in a cup of honey and leave in the fridge. Next day take a teaspoon, whenever the throat irritates.
- Take warm water and add one teaspoon of salt or tea to it. Gargle every few hours, but with warm water that is tolerably hot. Gargle every few hours, as it will do a world of good.
- If not salt, dissolve two tablets of Disprin in warm water. Gargle and swallow the tablets.
- If your voice gets hoarse, inhale steam three or four times a day.
- Drink herbal or tea made of *tulsi* (basil) leaves mixed with two or three black peppers and a bit of crushed ginger at least four to five times a day.
- Drink warm and clear soups.
- Drink warm water instead of cold water.
- If the cough in severe, take the patient to the bathroom, close the door and fill hot water in a tub to let the steam fill up the room. If it is 'croup', then put a kettle of water on a stove and let the patient inhale the steam.
- Camomile is a herb that is soothing to the throat and helps in putting one to sleep. It is useful when inhaled during cough, which is accompanied with catarrh.
- Take two tablespoons of fresh thyme or one tablespoon of dried thyme in a cup of hot water. Let is mix for five minutes. Strain it and drink with honey.
- In a cup of hot water, put 2 gms of dried marshmallow. Let it set for 10 minutes and strain the mixture. Drink three cups a day.
- Soak five almonds overnight. Remove their skin and grind into a paste. Add a little butter and sugar. Keep on licking it often to suppress dry cough.
- Drink hot milk with honey to soothe the throat at bedtime.
- Drink hot tea with lemon and raspberry jam as often as possible.
- Add half a teaspoon of powdered ginger, a piece of clove and cinnamon powder to a cup of boiling water and drink.

Home Remedies

- To keep the chest warm, rub camphor or menthol.
- Take one part of mustard powder and two parts of flour in a bowl. Make into a paste by adding water. Spread the paste on a towel and fold the towel. Rub petroleum jelly on your chest and then place the poultice on top. Keep checking in between to see that the poultice is not too hot as to burn the skin.
- Steam inhalation of turmeric dissolved in water is good for controlling cough.
- In case of whooping cough, take 5mls. of juice of *tulsi* (basil) leaves in 10 ml of pure honey to give to a baby who has cough.
- In case of whooping cough, mix three parts of garlic juice with five parts of pure honey and give to the baby daily three times a day. In case the cough is accompanied with a fever of 101°F or more and the joints pain, or there is problem in swallowing, then consult a doctor.

27 Dandruff

Dandruff refers to the condition of hair when shiny, silky scales separate out from the scalp. Growing hair and maintaining it is not an easy job. Acute dandruff causes scratching along with a burning and itching feeling. The dandruff flakes are rough and have no discharge. Though it can occur at any age, it is generally the young who are affected by it.

Doctors believe that dandruff is the result of either too much or too little oil being produced by the sebaceous glands in the scalp. Dandruff refers to the outer layers of dead skin.

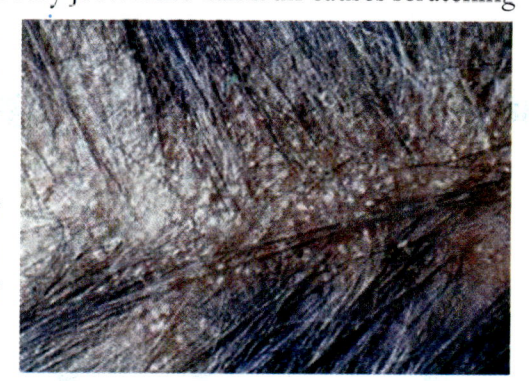

The condition can be due to a number of causes like stress, overactive sebaceous glands and seborrhoeic dermatitis when a scaly rash affects the face, the chest and the scalp.

Home Remedies

- One part of sandalwood mixed with three parts of lemon juice should be shaken in a bottle and applied to the scalp.
- A mixture of *neem* oil and camphor can be applied before washing the hair.
- Spread fresh yoghurt on the scalp and leave for an hour before rinsing. The bacteria in the yoghurt keep the yeast in check.
- The hair should be brushed vigorously three times a day to facilitate blood circulation in the scalp.
- Drink one or two teaspoon of flaxseed oil for at least three months before the results begin to show. Flaxseeds also guard against heart disease.

Home Remedies

- Dilute seven drops of tea-tree oil in one teaspoon of olive or grapeseed oil and apply to the scalp before leaving overnight. Wash off with a shampoo the next morning.
- Mix one part of water with one part of apple cider vinegar and apply as a rinse after shampooing your hair.
- Soak *amla* (Indian gooseberry) in water overnight. Boil it the next morning and add an equal amount of yoghurt to it. Apply on the scalp and leave for an hour before washing the scalp.
- Mix coconut oil with lemon juice and apply.
- Pour one cup of boiling water over a teaspoon of rosemary and let it set. Strain it and rinse you hair with it every day.
- Add a handful of crushed bay leaves to a litre of hot water and let it steep for half an hour. Strain it. Cool and apply on your hair. Leave for an hour and rinse with water.
- Make a dandruff rinse with two teaspoons of golden seal mixed in a cup of boiling water. Strain and cool. Use it as a rinse any time of the day.
- Two tablespoons of fenugreek seeds soaked overnight and ground into a paste should be applied and left for an hour before washing.
- Both the tops and roots of beet are boiled in water and massaged into the scalp.
- Wash your scalp and hair with two tablespoons of green gram powder.
- The juice of snake gourd is useful in treating dandruff.
- Avoid tea, coffee, pickles and processed foods.

28

Dark Complexion/ Sunburn

In India and in most Asian and Middle Eastern countries, dark skin is considered a bane as people crave for a fair skin, which is considered a plus point in the scale of beauty. Dark skin signifies excess of melanin, a pigment in the skin. Extraordinary amounts of melanin can lead to hyper pigmentation, making the skin look dark, blemished and patchy.

Dark skin is normally hereditary as it is handed down the generations, or it can be due to liver disorder, or a skin disease called *Lichen simplex chronicus* that causes severe itching. Moreover, in people working outdoors for long hours and getting over-exposed to the sun, which emits ultraviolet rays, the skin gets tanned. At times very delicate skin on sudden exposure to the sun for two to three days continuously turns red like a boiled lobster, causing significant pain, swelling and soreness. Repeated sunburn makes the skin age more quickly and increases the risk of skin cancer. Fair-complexioned people are more prone to sunburn.

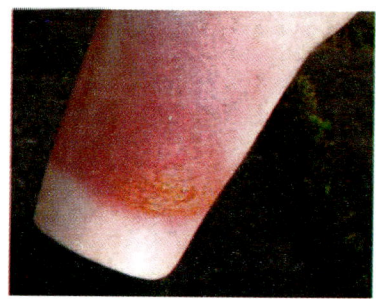

Precautions

- Limit your exposure to the sun by not going out in the afternoon.
- Carry an umbrella to guard against the sun's rays.
- Drink plenty of water, eat fresh fruits and maintain a well-balanced diet. Use a good quality sun cream when going outdoors.

Home Remedies

- Make a paste of sandalwood and turmeric powder and rub it lightly over the sunburned area at least twice or thrice a day.
- A daily intake of one teaspoon of sandalwood and turmeric proves beneficial.
- Splash cold water on the face and hands or other uncovered parts of the body.
- Apply lime juice to remove the tan as lime juice is a natural bleach.
- Place slices of raw potatoes or tomatoes on the affected area, as they help to reduce the blemishes on the skin.
- Make a paste of one teaspoon of honey, a teaspoon of lemon juice, a teaspoon of milk powder and half a teaspoon of almonds. Apply this on the face and leave for half and hour. Wash off with plain water. This pack removes the tan and brings shine to the skin.
- Dried orange peels (powdered) mixed with curd help to reduce blemishes and scars. Do not use soap to wash off as plain tap water is enough.
- Make a paste of oatmeal, curd and tomato juice to apply on the dark, exposed areas of the body. Leave it for half an hour before washing the paste away with water.
- Apply cold compress on the darkened areas, if caused due to over-exposure to the sun. Keep the skin cool with ice or tap water as it will reduce the swelling by drawing the heat of the skin.
- Brew green tea and let it cool. Soak a piece of cloth in it and apply on the darkened skin. This will protect the skin against further damage from the sun's rays besides reducing inflammation of the skin.
- Rub gently a slice of cucumber over the sunburned area as it cools the skin and reduces the swelling.
- Mix two drops of peppermint oil in a cup of lukewarm water. Cool it with ice cubes and apply on the sunburned area.
- Soak four or five almonds overnight. Grind them into a paste by using milk. Apply on the face and leave it overnight. Do this daily once or twice a day to obtain favourable results.
- Make a paste with mint leaves and water and apply on the dark or burnt area.
- apply a mixture of grated tomato and lime juice on the face. Leave it on for half an hour before washing off.
- Soak a few sheets of brown paper or crepe paper in white or cider vinegar and lay them on the burnt areas till they are dry.

Home Remedies

- Break open a vitamin e capsule and apply it to the skin.
- Make a paste of barley, turmeric and yoghurt to apply on the dark or sunburned skin.
- Apply a coating of egg white, honey and witch hazel on the affected area.
- Toothpaste helps to cool down and soothe the burnt skin.
- Fair-skinned people can eat a paste of tomato as the lycopene in it protects the skin against the harmful ultraviolet rays.
- A tablespoon of green flour mixed with two teaspoons of raw milk and a few drops of lime juice help to lighten the dark skin.
- Grind fresh turmeric and mix it with a spoon of milk cream to apply on the face. Leave it on for half an hour before washing it off.
- Mix lemon juice, glycerine and rosewater and apply at night daily before going to bed.

29

Dark Underarms

Women and young girls often find it an embarrassment to wear sleeveless shirts or blouses if they have dark underarms. A number of causes are responsible for this malady, the principal ones being excessive friction on the skin due to tight-sleeved blouses and shirts, or due to excessive sweating, or shaving with a blunt blade, or use of strong perfumes, chemicals and deodorants.

Precautions

- Wear loose-fitting sleeves, especially in the underarm portion to allow entry of air.
- Use high quality deodorants or perfumes for applying in the armpits.
- Sprinkle talcum powder to ward off perspiration that attracts bacteria.
- Wash your armpits with soap and water.
- Wear cotton clothes as synthetic ones accumulate bacteria.

Home Remedies

- After a shower, rub baking soda on the armpits.
- Make a paste of one teaspoon of lime juice, one teaspoon of cucumber juice and a pinch of turmeric powder. Apply it on the armpits. Wash off after half an hour.
- Apply vitamin E oil on your armpits.
- Make a paste of one tablespoon of curd, one teaspoon of gram flour, a pinch of turmeric powder and a teaspoon of milk. Apply on the underarms and let it dry. Wash off with water.
- Use a deodorant, which suits your skin.

30

Depression

Depression is an emotional disorder in which feelings of sadness, utter misery, dejection, sorrow and all kinds of unpleasant memories manifest. The complexities of modern life, stress and strain, a divorce, a death, a career change can induce depression as you experience loss or lack of interest in the world around and also fatigue. Disturbed sleep is a frequent occurrence. Other symptoms include itching, nausea, agitation, impotence or frigidity, aches and pains in the body, lack of concentration and extreme mood swings.

Severe depression is accompanied by low body temperature, low blood pressure, hot flashes and shivering. Prolonged periods of anxiety or tension can cause mental depression.

Home Remedies

- The best cure is aerobic exercise, jumping, skipping or running till sweat builds up.
- Avoid coffee or cola as caffeine suppresses the serotonin production linked to depression.
- Avoid alcohol of any kind because it normally acts as a depressant.
- Vitamin B, phosphorus and potassium present in apple makes it an effective nerve tonic as it brings new energy and life into you.
- Cashew nuts, rich in vitamins of the B group, especially thiamine, stimulate the nervous system.
- Roots of asparagus are highly beneficial in depression.
- Mix cardamoms in tea and drink as it lifts depression.
- Lemon balm alleviates brain fatigue and cheers up the person.
- Magnesium supplements help to stimulate the tense nerves and relax a person.
- Get enough sleep.
- Chocolate is good for mood boost.

31

Diabetes

A metabolic disorder in which the body utilises the glucose completely or partially is called 'diabetes mellitus'. It is a life-long problem but can be kept under control by daily use of drugs, exercise and diet. In Ayurveda, it is known as *madhumeha,* i.e. passing of honey-like urine. The glucose level in the blood rises, as carbohydrates are not properly utilised due to deficiency of insulin.

There are two types of diabetes — Type 1 is insulin-dependent, where the pancreas fails to manufacture enough insulin. It occurs in childhood mostly and the patient needs insulin daily. In this type, weight loss is seen.

Type 2 or non-insulin-dependent diabetes mellitus occurs when the body cells become resistant to insulin. This is common in overweight people and those above 40 years of age. They can control their diabetes through regular exercise, proper diet and weight control.

The initial symptoms include increased thirst, excessive urination and increased appetite. In insulin-dependent diabetes, the person becomes weak, feels thirsty and excretes large quantities of urine. If not checked, the diabetic may lose consciousness and pass into a coma.

In non-insulin-dependent diabetes, excessive thirst and urine, tiredness, a feeling of pins and needles and blurred vision are experienced.

Diabetics suffer from recurrent boils and carbuncles, thrush and itching in the genital region because of high blood sugar levels in the urine. Wounds take long to heal.

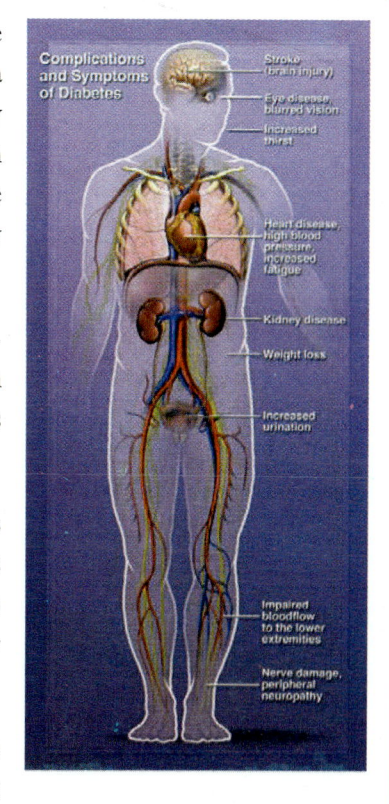

Precautions

- Keep away from fried and sugar-rich food.
- Avoid starchy food.
- A well-balanced diet should be taken.

Home Remedies

- *Karela* (bitter gourd) juice should be taken on an empty stomach.
- Fenugreek seeds soaked daily at night and taken in the morning prove useful.
- *Amla* (Indian gooseberry) juice mixed with a bit of turmeric powder maintains the sugar level.
- *Jamun* (Indian berry) juice mixed with a cup of bitter-gourd juice taken daily stimulates the cells that secrete the hormone insulin in the pancreas. This reduces the blood sugar.
- Cinnamon powder may help a lot in Type 2 diabetes as it improves the ability to respond to insulin, thus normalising the sugar levels.
- Grapefruit eaten liberally would help in control of diabetes. If you have a high sugar count, eat three grapefruits daily.
- Soak Bengal gram in water as the water extract taken daily helps in improvement of fasting blood sugar levels.
- Tender leaves of mango tree should be soaked in water overnight and their juice extracted next day. This should be taken every morning to control early diabetes.
- Seeds of parsiane taken in a spoon with half a cup of water increase the body's insulin and cures diabetes.
- String beans, cucumber, onion, and garlic should be eaten often.
- Juice of *satavar* mixed with an equal amount of milk is helpful in controlling sugar in blood.

32

Diarrhoea

Eating food from vendors or drinking poor quality water encourages viruses, bacteria and protozoa to attack your stomach, making your insides rumble and the bowel to leak. Diarrhoea, in other words, refers to frequent passage of loose or watery unformed stools.

Diarrhoea may be acute or chronic. The small intestine gets its liquid content from the diet and from the secretions of the stomach, liver, pancreas and the intestines. If water is not absorbed or is excreted in excess, the urge to defecate arises often. The body loses valuable fluids and electrolytes in the process. Diaorrhoea, that lasts for days or weeks, suggests an irritable bowel syndrome, leading to dehydration. This is a case of chronic diarrhoea.

Precautions

- Take drinks like orange juice and colas as they keep the bacteria in check.
- If you find you get diarrhoea after drinking milk or a dairy product, then try substitutes like soya milk. Drink water that is boiled.
- Stay away from artificial and natural sweeteners in strawberries, cherries, plums and peaches.
- Wash your hands with soap and water before you prepare food.
- Do not take too much of vitamin C as it causes diarrhoea.
- Avoid roughage in vegetables and fruits as it causes diarrhoea.

Home Remedies

- Eat liberal doses of yoghurt as the bacteria in it are carried to the intestine, speeding up recovery.

Home Remedies

- Peel and crush two cloves of garlic. Add two teaspoons of brown sugar and boil in a cup of water. Drink two or three times a day. Garlic is a potent anti-bacterial and is an ancient Chinese treatment.
- Ground *Isabgol* (psyllium seeds) and eat it as it will soak up the excess fluid.
- Drink black tea with sugar as it will dehydrate the body. It at also contains tannin that reduces intestinal inflammation.
- Make blackberry tea with dried blackberry leaves. Put these in boiling water. Simmer for 10 minutes and strain. Drink one cup several times to control diarrhoea.
- Prepare an electrolyte by stirring half a teaspoon of salt and four teaspoons of sugar in a litre of water. Add orange or lemon juice. During the day, drink at least a litre of this electrolyte.
- If your diarrhoea is light, start drinking soft drinks to restore the fluid level.
- Avoid fruit juices but take carrot soup by boiling carrots in water and making a soft puree of it. Take a tablespoon of it every two hours.
- Avoid roughage but take plenty of yoghurt, as it helps to speed up recovery.
- After removing fat from curd by churning it, extract the buttermilk and take with a pinch of salt.
- Take fenugreek leaves and cook as a vegetable and eat with buttermilk.
- Dry and fresh ginger should be powdered with rock salt. A quarter teaspoon of it is taken with a small piece of jaggery as often as possible. It aids in digestion by stimulating the gastro-intestinal tract.
- One teaspoon of fresh mint juice mixed with lime juice can be taken thrice daily.
- A teaspoon of juice extracted from drumstick leaves mixed with a teaspoon of honey can be taken with tender coconut water.
- Pomegranate juice should be taken to control diarrhoea.
- Fresh turmeric juice or a teaspoon of turmeric powder can be taken in a cup of buttermilk.
- Roast sesame seeds in a frying pan and grind them into a powder. Mix the powder in a teaspoon of *ghee* (clarified butter) and take it with boiled goat's milk.
- Dry the mango seeds. Powder them and take the powder with or without honey twice a day.

Home Remedies

- Apply cold compress or take a cold tub-bath.
- Starchy liquids like arrowroot water, barley water and coconut water are beneficial and so are bananas and garlic. Bananas contain pectin that encourages the growth of beneficial bacteria. Garlic is a powerful germ killer. Cooked or baked apples are also good.
- A teaspoon of charred parboiled rice with a glass of buttermilk should be taken after every half hour.
- Boil one teaspoon of fennel seeds in a cup of water until water is half its quantity. Take two to three teaspoons of this many times daily.

33

Dry or Oily Skin

The skin is the outermost layer, which needs to be protected against the vagaries of the weather. Skin can be either oily, normal or dry. With the beginning of every new season, the skin turns dry or oily.

Oily skin can be attended to by washing it often with soap and water and desisting from drinking aerated drinks, or eating fatty and oily foodstuffs. It is dry skin, which needs a lot of management with gentle cleansing, regular stimulation of the skin by massaging with generous quantities of oil and moisture. Washing with ordinary soap will deplete the skin's oil content, while the use of a moisturiser will increase the water content, imparting it a soft, moist look. A bath with a glycerine soap, like pears or dove, followed by an application of baby oil and a nourishing cream every night will keep the skin soft and prevent formation of crows' feet and lines around the mouth.

It is particularly during the winter months that the dry air causes the skin to become flaky, itchy, cracked and rough. The skin gets a parched look due to its inability to retain water. It feels 'tight' and uncomfortable after washing, so some moisturiser has to be used on it.

It is the exposed parts like the face, the hands and feet which suffer the most; particularly the hands as they produce the least amount of essential and protective sebum. The skin looks dull, especially around the eyes and corners of the mouth, giving expression lines on these areas.

Precautions

- Stay out of the sun as it can burn the skin.
- Drink plenty of water to keep yourself well hydrated.
- Avoid fried foods because hot oil leads to production of free radicals that have a harmful effect on the skin.

Precautions

- Do not drink aerated drinks or eat sugar, chocolates, French fries, etc.
- Avoid coffee and liquor.
- Sleep for seven to eight hours regularly.
- Exercise your limbs as it boosts blood circulation and cleanses the skin from within.

Home Remedies

- Every morning apply on the face and hands a skin cleanser made of one egg yolk, one teaspoon of orange juice, one teaspoon of olive oil and a few drops of rosewater and lime juice.
- Soak a piece of flannel in milk and spread the flannel on the dry skin for some time. After half an hour, wash off the milk with tap water.
- Add two cups of Epsom salts to a bucket of water and take a bath with it. You can even rub Epsom salts on the rough areas to exfoliate the skin.
- Apply aloe vera to help the dry skin to heal more quickly.
- Make a face mask with an egg, a teaspoon of honey, half a teaspoon of olive oil and rosewater and apply on the face. Wash off after some time.
- Use mineral water instead of tap water to wash the skin.
- Pour two cups of colloidal (ground into a powder) oatmeal in a tub of lukewarm water and take a bath in it.
- Drink plenty of water.
- Apply *neem*-leaf extract on dry lips.
- Leave on some aloe vera gel on dry lips.
- Take a saline bath.
- Eat plenty of vitamin A-rich food, like carrots, tomatoes and green leafy vegetables.
- Apply a thin line of *desi ghee* (clarified butter) on your lips to avoid chapped lips.
- Mash half an avocado with lemon juice and spread it over the cleansed skin. Leave it

Home Remedies

for half an hour before washing off with cold and warm water alternately.
- Prepare an easy skin pack by mashing a ripe banana with a fork and spreading it over the face, throat and hands for some time before washing it off with lukewarm water.
- Add a drop of coconut or mustard oil to a bucket of water before bathing as it helps to moisturise the skin.
- Use Fuller's earth (*multani mitti*) on your face and wash off after half an hour.
- use a mixture of calendula oil, vitamin E oil and aloe vera on the hands before bedtime.
- Blend together one teaspoon of green clay and one teaspoon of raw honey before applying on the face, avoiding the eyes. Leave it on for half an hour before washing your face with water.
- Mix 40 gms of orange flowers, rosewater, distilled water, and 5 gms of glycerine, alcohol and colon water. Use this as a face wash.
- Mash strawberries and apply the juice on the skin for a while.
- Melt some yeast in water and apply on your face.
- Grind an onion and rub the juice on the face.

34

Ear Infection

The ear is made up of three parts — the outer ear, the middle ear and the inner ear. Ear infection is commonly seen in boys in the winter season. There can be itching in the infected ear followed by discharge, fever and reduction in hearing. Dizziness or vomiting can occur in extreme cases. The main cause is blockage of the Eustachian tube, which runs from the middle ear to the back of the throat. It allows fluids to drain. The common cold virus can cause the fluid to accumulate, causing pain.

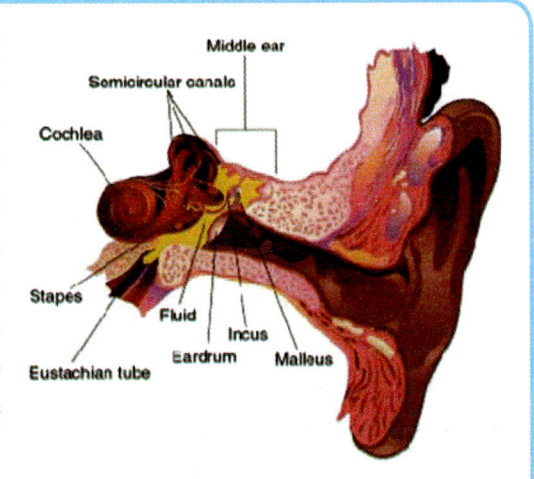

Frequent swimming or water exposure can cause infection by bacteria. At times it could be allergic infection.

Precautions

- Avoid people suffering from a cold or cough.
- Do not go near a person smoking a cigarette.
- Do not hear loud noises.

Home Remedies

- Warm a teaspoon of olive or baby oil, or mustard oil, and test the temperature by putting a drop on the wrist. Then put a few drops in the ear only if the drop is found tolerable.

Home Remedies

- Try drinking spicy chicken soup or a bowl of chillies as that will make the mucus flow out, helping the ears to drain.
- Gulp down plenty of water as gulping helps the Eustachian tubes to open up.
- Gargle with warm salt water to increase blood circulation in the Eustachian tube.
- Put a few drops of garlic juice in the infected ear.
- Take vitamin C and zinc to reduce ear infection.
- Eat one or two raw cloves of garlic every day or take a garlic capsule.
- If a wax plug forms in the ear, it can cause aching or ringing in the ears, hearing loss and balance problem. Use a solvent to soften the wax and then take an earwash to flood out the gunk.
- Gently massage the area behind the earlobe to loosen the wax or tug the earlobe while opening and closing your mouth.
- Mix equal parts of surgical spirit and white vinegar in a clean ear-dropper and put few drops in your ear. Tilt your head to the opposite side to let the drops stay inside.

Eczema

Eczema means 'boiling over' of the skin and is characterised by eruptions accompanied with itching, redness, flaking and tiny blisters. There are several types of eczema — 'atopic' eczema occurs in people with a family history of allergies or asthma and is marked by an acute flare up of fluid-filled blisters. If scratched, it leads to bacterial infection. Another type of eczema is called 'contact dermatitis' and is caused on coming into contact with an irritating substance, like a detergent or cosmetic or a chemical. It can be caused by stress or a combination of stress and allergic reaction.

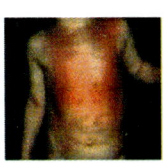

Precautions

- Avoid contact with detergents; instead use gloves to wash hands.
- Avoid use of synthetic clothes as they prevent evaporation of perspiration.
- Eat a piece of watermelon piece often.
- Avoid spicy foods.
- Bitter gourd and *neem* flowers are helpful.
- Pure turmeric is externally useful and can be dissolved in milk and drunk.

Home Remedies

- Make a paste with the bark of *neem* tree and boil in water. This prevents secondary infection and itching.
- Put a few drops of *neem* oil in a cup of warm milk with sugar and drink daily for 40 days.
- Apply the paste of *neem* bark on the affected area.

Home Remedies

- Add one teaspoon of camphor to a teaspoon of sandalwood paste and apply on the eczema.
- Rub a nutmeg on a stone slab with a little water to make a paste, which should be applied to the affected area.
- Crush *doob* grass, *harar, sendha namak* (rock salt), *chokkar* (wheat bran) and *tulsi* (basil) leaves in milk and apply on the affected area for six weeks. Good results will be seen.
- Mix one teaspoon of comfrey root, a teaspoon of white oak bark, a teaspoon of slippery elm bark and two cups of water. Boil and wash the affected area with it.
- Zinc taken orally and applied on the affected skin is effective.
- Use pine-tar soap to wash the skin.
- Apply a camomile or witch hazel cream to reduce skin inflammation.

36 Fever

When the body temperature rises above normal, it is called 'fever'. Often fever is a symptom of other diseases. It is also characterised by disturbance in the normal functioning of the body. The normal temperature is 36.9°C or 98.4°F or a bit above or below. When it is high, the person's face is hot to touch, the eyes look glazed, the head pains, he feels thirsty and a feeling of lethargy sets in. As the fever rises, the pulse beats increase, shivering occurs and a copious flow of concentrated urine follows.

The real cause of fever is accumulation of morbid matter in the system and which is toxic and needs to be removed. Fever acts as a warning signal that something is wrong with the food consumed.

Precautions

- Take rest as undue strain may aggravate the fever.
- Avoid cold and sour food.
- As the body becomes hydrated, take plenty of water and liquids.
- Citrus juice is good as it helps your body to fight the infection.
- Do cold water sponging if the temperature is high.

Home Remedies

- Boil some basil leaves in water and give to the patient with half a cup of milk. A teaspoon of sugar and powdered *elaichi* (cardamom) can be added before boiling.
- Drink a cup of hot ginger tea by boiling ginger in water and straining it.

Home Remedies

- Sprinkle cayenne pepper on food as the capsacin in it will make you sweat and lower the temperature.
- Warm your feet in hot water. Soak a pair of socks in cold water, squeeze the water out and put them on before going to bed. Over the wet socks, pull up a pair of dry woollen socks. By drawing blood to the feet, the blood circulation is increased.
- To fresh leaves of *neem* add honey and drink thrice a day.
- In a tub add two teaspoon of mustard powder to hot water and soak your feet in it.
- The herb elderflower boiled in water and steeped will help you sweat and lower your temperature.
- Fenugreek seeds soaked in water and made into tea for drinking is a soothing drink in fever.
- Put half a teaspoon of saffron in boiling water and drink often till your temperature recedes.
- Soak raisins in water, crush them and extract the pulp. Add half a teaspoon of lime juice and drink this mixture twice a day.
- Fresh juice of apricots mixed with glucose is a cooling drink for bringing down fever.
- Grapefruit, orange, bloodwort or hogweed prepared by steeping in water helps to lower the body temperature.
- Apply a cold wet cloth to the forehead to bring down temperature.
- Drink heated coke with lime juice for lowering the fever.
- Wrap the body of the patient in a linen piece soaked in cold water. Cover the body with a thin blanket. Do this every three hours when the temperature is high or give the patient a cold-water bath and wrap him in woollens.

Gum Trouble

The commonest form of gum disease in a mild inflammation of the margins of the gum. Known as 'gingivitis', it is caused by formation of plaque by unfriendly bacteria on the teeth, making the gums red and sore. If not treated soon, the gum recedes and swells to begin bleeding. This is called 'peridontitis' when pus develops and the teeth loosen and fall out.

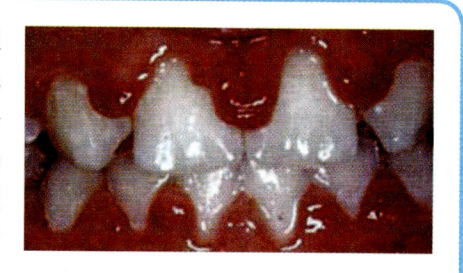

Precautions

- Do not use a hard brush for brushing the teeth.
- Gargle with saline water.

Home Remedies

- Place a wet teabag on the painful area as the tannic acid acts as an astringent and shrinks the swollen tissues.
- Apply the pack to the cheek, close to the painful gum. It will reduce swelling.
- In acute pain, chew a clove or apply clove oil.
- Massage your gums with coconut oil.
- Calendula helps to reduce gum inflammation.
- Rinse your mouth with camomile tea as it is effective against gingivitis.
- Dab your gums with a paste of soda bicarbonate and water as soda helps to kill germs.

38

Hair Problems

Hair that is dry, frizzy at the ends, brittle and lacks lustre is called 'dry hair'. Though it has no life, just as the fingernails, each strand has an outer layer of cells that protects the inner hair shaft. If the layer gets damaged, the hair loses its sheen and moisture to get frayed and lifeless.

Hair that is oily without being oiled looks lank, dirty and sticky to your head. In this case, the oil-producing glands lying beneath the surface of the skin and called 'sebaceous glands' secrete too much sebum, which is a mixture of fatty acids that protects your scalp. Heredity, stress, secretion of male hormone called androgen or a poor diet is responsible for oily or greasy hair.

Grey hair is hair that starts whitening or greying at an early age, causing embarrassment to both males and females. Losing hair is a natural phenomenon and it is normal for 20-100 strands to fall off. After a few months, new hair will grow to replace the fallen hair. At times, acute hair fall occurs in childbirth, surgery, long bout of fever, or a sudden emotional shock. Use of anti-cancer drugs also causes hair loss.

Premature greying of hair runs in the family and can occur even at the age of 20. It is caused by loss of melanin, a pigment, from the hair. Vitiligo or skin pigmentation as also Alopecia areata, where the hair loss is in a patch, cause early greying.

Precautions

- Use a proper mild shampoo for washing the hair once if the hair is dry, twice if the hair is greasy.
- Do not comb wet hair vigorously as their tensile strength is less when wet and they break easily.

Precautions

- Keep your hair-comb clean.
- Trim the hair once every three months.
- Do not wash hair with hot water.

Home Remedies

- *Dry hair*
- Use a baby shampoo to wash dry hair as it is the mildest form of shampoo.
- Peel an avocado, extract the juice by grating it and mix it in wheat germ oil and jojoba oil. Massage this into your hair, leave for half an hour and rinse with water.
- Rub mayonnaise in the hair, leave it on for an hour and wash out.
- Chop fresh buckwheat in two cups of boiling water, cool and smear on the hair. Wash after half an hour.
- Put lemon juice and sea-water in the hair and sit in the sun for 20 minutes. Wash the hair.
- Mix lemon juice and camomile, wet your hair and apply the mixture on the hair. Stay in the sun for a while and wash the hair.
- Make a conditioner with 60 gms of olive oil, 60 gms of aloe vera gel and six drops each of rosemary and sandalwood oils. Olive oil is an emollient and imparts a sheen to the hair. Leave the mixture on for an hour and wash.
- Take plenty of fruits and vegetables rich in vitamin b as it makes the hair stronger.
- *Oily hair*
- After washing your hair with a lanolin-rich shampoo, rinse the hair with rosemary tea prepared by using rosemary in boiling water.
- Rinse your hair with a few drops of vinegar mixed in water as vinegar is acidic and de-greases the oily hair.
- Rub the lemon rind or lemon halves in your hair, leave for an hour and wash off with cool water.
- *Grey hair*
- Grey hair is normally dry hair, so follow the remedies described for dry hair.

Home Remedies

- Soak henna, coffee powder and *amla* in boiling water and wash your hair regularly every week with this lotion to halt greying.
- Soak *amla* (Indian gooseberry) in as iron griddle at night and next morning, apply the paste on the hair and leave for an hour. Wash off with water.
- Soak henna and coffee powder in boiling water and leave it on the hair for two to three hours. Wash off with a shampoo. The hair will turn orangish-red in colour on regular use.
- *Hair fall*
- Eat a protein-rich diet to stop hair fall.
- Brush your hair at least 50 times, if not 100, to circulate the blood in the scalp.
- Soak hibiscus rosa (red shoeflower) in water and massage on the scalp. Leave for an hour and wash.
- Massage warm olive oil, or almond oil, or coconut oil, and leave it overnight. Next morning, shampoo your hair.
- Apply the pulp of *amla* and mango together and leave it on the scalp for one hour before washing off.
- Keep your hair clean and the stomach clean too so that the hair does not fall due to poor health.
- Take a teaspoon of *amla* powder and Ayurvedic *Bhringaraj* three times a day with water to stop hair fall.

39

Headache

A traffic jam in a crowded place, or an argument with your boss or spouse, is enough provocation to give you a headache. Headache could be due to a multiple number of causes, like a tumour or high blood pressure, but in most cases the cause is a tense and uneasy mind. A severe form of headache is migraine, which is more frequent in women and is accompanied by pounding arteries, throbbing veins in the head, nausea and sensitivity to light. Affecting mostly males, cluster headaches, which occur often at night, are triggered by smoking or drinking. Such a headache comes in groups or 'clusters' followed by periods of remission.

Precautions

- Allow plenty of fresh air to enter the room. Do not sit or sleep in a closed, stuffy room.
- When sleeping, do not cover your head with a quilt or sheet for it prevents oxygen from entering your nose and you get a splitting headache.
- Sleep at least eight hours a day or else you may go in for a headache.
- Some people get a headache if they sleep for too long as it gives a heavy head, making them feel miserable.
- Regular exercise like walking, jogging and swimming works wonders as fresh air quickens the blood circulation.
- Deep breathing is a good stress-buster when tension headaches are caused.
- Eat your meals on time as some people suffer from a drop in blood sugar, which may result in a headache. Take small and frequent meals.
- Protect your eyes from the glare of lamps, or the sun, or too much attention on the TV screen, or on the computer screen. Look away every now and then to protect the eyes and prevent the onset of a headache.

Precautions

- Avoid late nights. Painting the town red at night may give a splitting headache the next day.
- Avoid alcohol and if taken, it may be a peg or two, else a hangover accompanied with a headache can spoil your next morning.
- Keep away from loud music or noisy gatherings if susceptible to a bout of headache.
- Keep away from smoke-filled rooms, be it smoke of tobacco or a religious event where clarified butter, incense, etc. Are used to pour into a lighted fire.

Home Remedies

- Soak fresh henna leaves in water for half an hour, make a paste and apply over the forehead to get relief.
- Make a paste of cinnamon powder after grinding the cinnamon. This can be applied over the temples and forehead.
- Soak your feet in hot water. It will make your head feel better. Warm feet will draw the blood from the head to the feet and ease pressure in the head.
- If the headache is severe, add mustard powder to the hot water in which the feet are soaked.
- *Jalebis* (an Indian sweetmeat) can be immersed in warm milk for a few minutes and taken two to three times a day.
- Do not consume cold food items like curd, ice cream, cold drinks or bathe in cold water during a headache.
- Eat plenty of green vegetables, legumes, whole cereals and milk.
- Apply a hot compress or hot water bottle wrapped in a towel to the forehead to relax the knotted-up muscles in the area.
- If the headache is at the back of the neck, then use a cold compress by wrapping ice cubes in a piece of flannel and placing on the sensitive nerves in the back of the neck.
- Soak your hands in iced water and close and open your wrists in it. The cold water will narrow down the dilated blood vessels.
- A strong cup of coffee can provide relief at times.
- Grind half a teaspoon of ginger and mix in a glass of water. Drink it or dissolve ginger paste in hot water. Let it become lukewarm before drinking it up. Ginger is

Home Remedies

very effective in curing migraine. It not only helps to curb nausea, ginger affects the prostaglandins, which are hormone-like substances that cause inflammation of blood vessels in the head.

- Add a few cloves to basil tea and drink.
- Pour a cup of boiling water over a teaspoon of dried rosemary and let it set. Strain and drink.
- Gently massage lavender oil on the forehead and temples and lie down to relax.
- Peppermint oil can be rubbed on the forehead as it helps to relax the nerves.
- In a vapouriser, add three or four drops of lavender oil and another three or four drops of peppermint oil and inhale.
- Soak a headband or scarf in vinegar and tie it around your head, as it will reduce the flow of blood to the scalp and relieve the pain in the head.
- Take powdered ginger as soon as you fear a bout of migraine setting in.
- If the headache persists, then get your eyes checked by an optimetrist or consult a neurophysician for a tumour in the brain, or it could be due to sinusitis and blocked nose.

40

Hiccups

A common belief to justify repeated hiccups is that someone is remembering you. How far this is correct is debatable but what is known is that it involves sudden contractions of the diaphragm that bring in crowing sounds. Temporary relief can be obtained by pressing the centre of the moustache region or drinking a glass of water. These are measures which may provide relief or not, but they help to hide your embarrassment. The cause may lie in the lower part of the food-pipe or the stomach, or the pancreas. No one really knows what causes them. Eating of certain foods or drinking excessive alcohol, or swallowing air, or downing a fizzy drink, or getting excited can also cause hiccups.

Home Remedies

- Plug your ears with your fingers till a count of 10. This helps because this way the vagus nerve is plugged temporarily when the ears are closed as the nerve ends in the ear.
- Just try to think of some of the people who could be remembering you and the hiccups might stop.
- Drink a glass of water slowly.
- Hold your breath till a count of 10 or take a paper bag and breathe into it for a short time. This way the carbon dioxide level in your body will rise and relieve you of hiccups.
- Press the palm of your hand with the thumb of the other hand as hard as possible, or press the ball of your left thumb between the thumb and forefinger of the right. This distraction affects your nervous system and puts an end to the hiccups.
- Press the soft areas behind your earlobes, just below the base of the skull. This sends a 'relax' signal through the vagus nerve, leading to the diaphragm area.
- Swallow crushed ice or dry bread.

Home Remedies

- Stick your tongue out as it stimulates the opening (the glottis) between the vocal cords.
- Cup your hands over your nose and mouth, while breathing normally.
- put one teaspoon of sugar or honey in a cup, stir it in warm water and swallow it.
- Crush one cardamon, mix it with honey and suck it.
- *Kulatha* in the form of soup is very effective.
- Cut a slice of lemon and suck it.
- Swallow a teaspoon of cider vinegar.
- Take a spoon of ice cream and swallow it in bits.
- Lie on the bed on your stomach with head turned and arms hanging down. Take a deep breath, hold it and exhale slowly. Repeat this a number of times.

41

High Blood Pressure/ Hypertension

Hypertension refers to high blood pressure in an individual and depends on his age, physical activity, mental tension, sex, family history and also diet. In a majority of cases, no specific underlying cause can be found. High blood pressure means that your heart is working more than it should to pump blood and your arteries are stressed. It is risky. If you do not lower it, you face the risk of suffering from a stroke, heart attack, kidney disease, or other deadly illnesses. High blood pressure means that the systolic pressure is 140 or above and the diastolic is 90 or higher. It signs and symptoms include chronic headache, palpitations, nose bleeds, fatigue, shortness of breath, frequent urination, diseased kidneys, hormonal disorders, mental tension, blurred vision, flushed face and a ringing sound in the ears. It is a warning to control your blood pressure. At times, people get so nervous to get their blood pressure checked that they experience a sudden rise in blood pressure and this is known as 'white coat hypertension'.

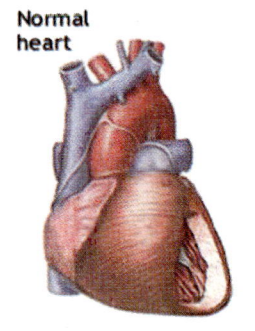

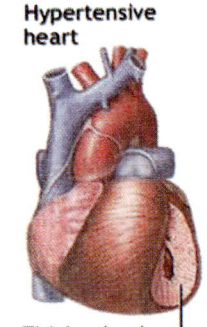

Precautions

- Cut down on salt intake.
- Learn to relax and avoid tension.
- Do vigorous exercise.
- Reduce alcohol intake.
- Avoid cooking in hydrogenated oils.

Home Remedies

- Take a teaspoon of almond oil at bedtime with a cup of milk.
- Make a paste of crushed garlic and take it with buttermilk.
- Take a tablespoon of *Sarpagandha* thrice a day.
- Eat at least five servings of fruits and vegetables per day as they contain potassium, magnesium and fibre, which keep the arteries healthy.
- Eat a bowl of porridge daily, as it is fibre-rich that contains beta-glucan.
- If overweight, try to lose at least 5 kg to reduce blood pressure.
- Do brisk exercise for half an hour.
- Learn to meditate.
- Eat a clove of garlic a day.
- To increase the intake of omega-3 fatty acids, take fish like mackerel and salmon.
- Vegetarians can take one tablespoon of flaxseed oil daily by mixing it in a fruit juice or into salad dressing.
- Mix equal amounts of onion juice and honey. Take two tablespoons once daily for at least three weeks.
- Eat a papaya on an empty stomach daily for a month. At least for two hours after eating the papaya, avoid eating anything else.
- In case of low blood pressure, a glass of beetroot juice should be taken twice a day for two weeks.

42 Insomnia

The word 'insomnia' denotes 'lack of sleep'. It is the relative inability to sleep that includes difficulty in falling asleep or remaining asleep, awakening early or a combination of all three complaints. Such sleep deprivation makes you feel groggy and irritable the next morning.

The single symptom of prime occurrence is difficulty in falling asleep. This could lead to changes in sleep patterns, lapse of memory, lack of concentration during the day, emotional instability, loss of coordination and a confused state of mind.

The most common causes of insomnia are overwork, constipation, emotional stress, depression, pain or illness, over-excitement, use of medications like diuretics or decongestants, dyspepsia, a heavy meal before going to bed, or a cup of caffeine, or alcohol, or simply trying to sleep in a new place on a new bed. Even suppressed resentment, anger and bitterness, lack of exercise and sedentary lifestyle can cause insomnia.

Precautions

- Avoid salt as it interferes with sleep.
- Avoid flour products, sugar, cola, caffeine and fried foods.
- Unwind and relax by taking half an hour off before going to bed. Let go of everything and think of pleasant things.
- Read a book or a magazine, or listen to music, to soothe your nerves before retiring to bed.
- Take a stroll in fresh air to remove anxiety and tension.
- Soak under a shower or in a bathtub before you hit the sack.

Home Remedies

- Try drinking a glass of warm milk with a spoonful of honey and a sprinkling of cinnamon as it might act like a mild sedative.
- Have a banana or chicken before sleeping as these contain tryptophan, an amino acid that makes serotonin, which helps in sleeping.
- Take half a teaspoon of valerian tincture before retiring.
- Put one teaspoon of dried passion flower in a cup of boiling water. Leave to infuse for 10 minutes and drink before going to bed.
- Lavender is supposed to be a tranquilliser. Dilute it in olive oil and dab a little on your temples and forehead before you hit the pillow.
- Put a drop of jasmine oil on each of your wrists.
- Eat plenty of wholegrain cereals, pulses and nuts, which are a rich source of vitamin B or thiamine that helps the nerves to relax.
- Extract juice of four lettuce leaves or boil lettuce seeds in water till the juice is reduced by one-third. Drink it.
- Curd is a good sleep-inducer. Massage it on the head and go to sleep.
- Prepare a mixture of bottle-gourd juice and sesame oil to massage on the scalp every night.
- Tea made from aniseed and boiling water induces sleep. Strain and drink it.
- Honey has a hypnotic effect. Take two teaspoons of it in a cup of water.
- Douse your eyes with rosewater at night, add a drop of *ghee* (clarified butter) in the eyes and close your eyes to sleep.
- The herb, Rauwolfia is a valuable medicine for insomnia. The herb powder should be mixed with cardamom and eaten.
- Eat an early meal shortly before sunset.
- Read an uninteresting book before sleeping.
- Take a tablespoon of peanut butter before sleeping.
- Do *pranayama* or *yoga asanas* before sleeping. Meditation before going to bed is ideal.
- Extract juice from green coriander leaves and mix with water and sugar. Drink it before sleeping.
- Avoid a high-protein dinner at night.

43

Peptic Ulcers

Peptic ulcers in the digestive system are very common in middle-aged men and women, who suffer from acidity. Craters like sores occur in the lining of your stomach or the upper part of the small intestine, the duodenum. They occur when pepsin, a digestive enzyme, begins to digest your own tissues. The digestive juices erode the weak points of the lining of the digestive tract and create a sore area, which ultimately leads to ulcer formation.

It is generally caused by eating hot and spicy food, heavy drinking or smoking. Belching, bloating or pain is commonly felt. Black stool and nausea may be the common symptoms. Irregular and bad eating habits aggravate the condition. A burning pain is felt in the upper abdomen or below the ribs, particularly after eating a meal.

Precautions

- Avoid aspirin-based drugs as they cause bleeding in the stomach.
- Stop drinking tea, coffee or alcohol and eating *paan* (betel leaf), etc.
- Try to keeps yourself tension- and stress-free.

Home Remedies

- Daily intake of pure *ghee* (clarified butter) is rewarding.
- Banana with milk neutralises the excessive acidity caused due to gastric juices.
- Inner bark of the slippery elm helps to protect the stomach lining.
- Herbal tea of calendula, camomile or marshmallow help to soothe the irritated lining of the digestive tract.
- Chew and swallow a teaspoon of flaxseeds as they are soothing to the stomach.

Home Remedies

- Juice of aloe vera quells gastro-intestinal inflammation.
- Drink raw cabbage juice three times a day.
- Eat plenty of onions because the sulphur compounds in it neutralise acidity.
- Take honey often.
- Take plenty of turmeric in whatever food it is possible.
- Peppermint is anti-inflammatory and can relieve pain.
- Eat plenty of yoghurt.
- Be moderate in use of non-steroid, anti-inflammatory drugs like aspirin and Ibuprofen as they cause ulcer formation.
- Avoid tea and coffee as they increase stomach acids.
- Take milk whenever the burning feeling persists.
- *Amla* (Indian gooseberry) juice can be extracted and taken with some sugar.
- The powder of *harar* mixed with honey and *gur* (jaggery) is very effective.
- A decoction of parsley, *pipal*, *parval* (gourd) and honey can be taken for ulcers and acidity.
- Raw carrot juice or juice of spinach, beet and cucumber is beneficial.
- Goat's milk is considered highly useful in ulcer.
- Leaves of *Kalyana murangal* tree prove helpful in healing ulcers.

44

Skin Rash

Skin rash is usually an inflammation on the skin. Eruptions on the skin of the back are called 'back rash'. Skin rash could be due to allergic reaction or as a result of irritation of skin. Small red and itchy lumps form on the skin, causing a stinging sensation.

Though the causes could be many, the prime reasons are allergy to dyes and chemicals or a reaction to cosmetics, perfumes and soaps.

Precautions

- Do not scrub your skin.
- Avoid exposing the affected area to direct sunlight and hot water.
- Stop usage of any new cosmetic, or soap, or lotion.
- Use lukewarm water for washing and avoid hot water.

Home Remedies

- Apply ice on the area.
- Apply olive oil on the rash to provide relief.
- Drink camomile tea after the rash has cooled down.
- Make a poultice of dandelion, yellow dock root and *chapavral* to apply on rash.
- Put a cup of uncooked oatmeal in your bath-water and soak in a tub for better results.
- Apply baby oil on the rash.

45

Stomach Pain/ Indigestion

Abdomen pain may be due to indigestion, gas, acidity, infection in the stomach; it can originate from other parts too such as the chest and pelvic region. Also known as 'dyspepsia', initial pain is known as stomach pain but when aggravated, it becomes indigestion. It can cause heartburn due to the influx of stomach acids. It irritates the oesophagus and leaves a bitter or sour taste in the mouth.

This can be due to quick gulping of food without chewing properly, eating a rich and heavy meal, particularly before going to bed, consuming excess alcohol, smoking, ulcer, stress, anxiety, use of anti-inflammatory drugs or change in lifestyle.

The illness occurs largely due to inability to pass food through the digestive tract as smoothly as normally done. Sufferers can experience nausea, heartburn or flowing back of their stomach acids up to the oesophagus. There can be pain due to bloating of stomach. Burning is another sign.

Precautions

- Avoid fruit juices as they contain fructose, a natural sugar that causes abdominal pain.
- Do not eat and drink at the same time.
- Do not rush when eating food.
- Do not overeat even if tempted to do so.
- Avoid tea and coffee.
- Avoid rich, fatty or spicy food that irritates the stomach.

Home Remedies

- Lemon is the fruit of choice in indigestion. Add half a lemon to a glass of water with a bit of soda bicarbonate in it. Stir well and drink for instant relief.
- Before eating at a party or taking a heavy meal, eat two or three small pieces of ginger coated with a bit of salt. Even if you get tempted to eat more, the ginger will prevent indigestion.
- Massage your lower abdomen as this will push out the trapped wind and digestive juices towards their natural exit. This also dispels bloating and constipation.
- Drink a teaspoon of cider vinegar stirred in a half a glass of water after a highly rich meal.
- A cup of hot water eases indigestion.
- Warm ginger ale, or a lemonade, or Limca soothes an upset stomach.
- A piece of *hing* (asafoetida) should be warmed in *ghee* (clarified butter) and applied on the belly button.
- Better still would be to add a pinch of *hing* powder and *ghee* to boiled rice and mix well. If eaten before a regular meal, its daily usage ensures proper digestion and evacuation of bowels.
- Massage your stomach with two drops of garlic oil and half a cup of soya oil.
- Herbal tea prepared with blackberry, raspberry, mint and camomile is effective in indigestion.
- Every three to four hours drink tea prepared with mint leaves and water. Honey can be added after straining the mixture.
- Fennel tea is equally effective as mint tea.
- Peppermint oil soothes intestinal cramps and helps to reduce bloating of the stomach.
- Chew and swallow a teaspoon of fennel or caraway seeds. These seeds contain oil that soothes the spasms in the gut, relieves nausea and controls flatulence.
- Make an infusion with equal parts of caraway, fennel and anise seeds added to boiling water. Strain and drink before every meal.
- Eat your last big meal at least three hours before bedtime.
- Prepare a mixture of *ajwain* (caraway seeds), a pinch of salt and a few drops of lemon juice in lukewarm water. Drink it.
- Chew betel leaves with a few rock salt crystals.

Varicose Veins

Swollen blood vessels on your legs can hurt and look ugly too. The problem involves dilation of the blood vessels, which become knotted and painful. Veins are responsible for transporting blood towards your heart. They have valves which, if weak, cause blood to collect and stop flowing. The veins become lumpy and are very common during pregnancy. People who stand for long on their feet are more prone to face this problem.

Precautions

- Do not stand on your feet for long hours.
- Spare time for doing aerobic exercises.
- Gently massage your legs at the end of a long day.
- Do not cross your legs when sitting.
- Whenever possible, walk around rather than sitting or standing at one place.

Home Remedies

- Run hot and cold water over your legs to expand and contract the blood vessels and improve blood circulation.
- Wear elastic stockings to support the varicose veins.

Home Remedies

- Eat plenty of high fibre-rich foods like wheat from cereals, apples and pears and whole grains so that the bowels work and you do not get constipation, which can put pressure on your legs.
- Take horse chestnut twice a day.
- Take gout kola extract three times daily.
- Add lemon peel to citrus drinks or to your tea as it contains rutin, a flavonoid that prevents leakage from small blood vessels.
- Apply apple cider vinegar every evening on the veins. Shrinking of the swollen veins will be noticed.
- Take two teaspoons of black strap molasses daily orally.

47 Warts

Warts are caused by a virus called *Human papilloma virus*, which is contagious and spreads infection by touch or contact. Warts are harmless growths on the skin and can grow up to 6 mm in diameter. A small, horny lump marks the beginning of a wart formation. Sometimes warts appear singly and at others, in clusters. Generally they appear as a pale skin growth.

Verrucas or plantar warts on the feet can be so painful that walking becomes difficult.

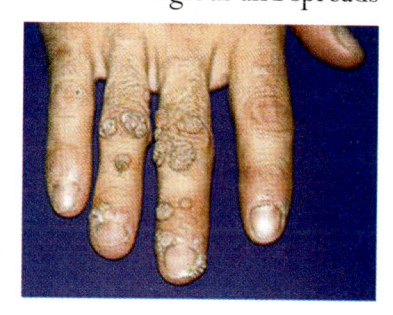

Home Remedies

- Castor oil should be applied regularly for a long time to soften the wart.
- An onion slice rubbed on the wart causes irritation and makes small warts disappear.
- Ayurvedic *Kasisadi tailam* should be applied externally on the wart.
- Apply oil extracted from the shell of cashew nut on the wart.
- Milk of papaya is effective in breaking the warts.
- Dissolve an aspirin tablet in a small drop of water and apply.
- Garlic cloves rubbed on the wart often and leave it on at night.
- Apply a drop of extract of grapefruit seeds.
- Apply the milky juice from the stems of figs and dandelion.
- Raw potato can be applied on the wart.
- Crush a vitamin E capsule and apply on the wart.
- Apply the juice of cauliflower on the wart.

Home Remedies

- Apply a cotton ball soaked in vinegar and tape it on the wart with an elastic sticking plaster.
- Peel a piece of bark from a birch tree, dampen it with water and tape it over your wart.
- Apply juice of lemon peel.
- Crush a few basil leaves and tape the extract over the warts with waterproof tape.
- For remaining verrucas or feet warts, soak your feet in hot water for about 15 minutes daily.

48 Worms

Worms and other intestinal parasites are commonly found in tropical and sub-tropical areas, affecting human beings. Children are more prone to be infected with them.

The symptoms include diarrhoea, foul breath, craving for food, headache, anaemia, restlessness and dark circles under the eyes.

Roundworms may cause nausea, loss of weight, fever, inflammation of intestine and lungs and irritability.

Threadworms cause intense itching in the area around the rectum, loss of weight, cough and fever.

Hookworms lead to anaemia and nutritional disorders and are introduced into the human system through food or water.

Precautions

- Do not walk barefooted.
- Do not eat under-cooked flesh food, or rotten or contaminated food.
- Wash your hands and nails to keep them clean.

Home Remedies

- Take a tablespoon of freshly ground coconut at breakfast, followed by 30-60 ml. of castor oil mixed in 250-370 ml. of lukewarm water after every three hours. Repeat the process till completely rid of the intestinal worms.

Home Remedies

- Garlic was used in ancient times by Chinese, Hindus, Greeks, Romans and Babylonians for expelling worms. Chew three to four cloves of garlic every morning.
- A small cup of grated carrot taken every morning will clear the body of threadworms.
- A tablespoon of papaya juice mixed with hot water destroys or expels intestinal worms. Papaya leaves contain carpacine, which mixed with boiling water, can be taken with honey.
- The bark of the root of pomegranate is also given as it is highly toxic to tapeworms.
- One tablespoon of pumpkin seeds should be peeled, crushed and infused in boiling water before drinking. It expels the tapeworms.
- The herb wormwood is an ancient cure for intestinal worms and was adopted by Greeks and Romans. It is used in India in Unani medicine to kill roundworms and tapeworms. Even the oil distilled from this plant kills worms.
- The leaves, bark, root-bark, fruit and flowers of *vasaka* tree also help in removing intestinal worms.
- Another remedy is to use the herb, calamus.
- A mixture of ginger and onion will help in deworming.

Female Problems

Though most illnesses affect both males and females, a few are confined essentially to the fairer sex and some to the stronger. Though it is not possible to cover all problems of females, a few important and most common ones will be discussed here and their remedies suggested.

49

Anaemia

Decrease in the quantity of haemoglobin or red blood cells (RBCs) causes anaemia, which is the most common ailment affecting human beings. In India, almost 20 per cent of women suffer from anaemia caused by iron deficiency. Loss of blood during menstruation is the main cause when excessive destruction of blood cells occurs, disallowing replacement by the bone marrow. This leads to insufficient production of hormones.

Vitamin-deficient anaemia and pernicous anaemia are caused due to inadequate supply of vitamin B12 and folic acid.

The patient complains of weakness, fatigue, loss of energy and dizziness. Premature wrinkles, listless and dull hair, tired eyes, shortness of breath, palpitations and poor memory are tell-tale signs of anaemia.

Precautions

- Avoid sour foods like curds and fried snacks.

Home Remedies

- Take meat, such as kidney and liver, as also dairy products, which are rich sources of vitamin B_{12}.
- Beet juice strengthens the body's resistance to disease, especially in children and teenagers as it contains potassium, calcium, phosphorus, sulphur, iron, iodine, protein, vitamins B_1, B2 and B6.
- Leaves of *methi* (fenugreek) help in blood formation and should be taken by girls at the onset of puberty and menstruation. The leaves are rich in iron.

Home Remedies

- Lettuce leaves too are rich in iron and should be taken raw.
- Green vegetables are rich in iron and folic acid and should be taken regularly.
- *Til* (sesame) seeds and jaggery are rich in iron.
- Ayurvedic *Triphala churan* should be taken with lukewarm water at bedtime.
- Spinach, soya beans, almonds, black grapes, plums, strawberries, raisins, carrots, radish, celery and tomatoes are rich in iron and should be eaten for treating anaemia.
- Cold-water baths taken twice daily or a hot Epsom salt-bath stimulates the production of red cells.
- Deep breathing exercises, walking and yogic *asanas* are helpful in this regard.
- Cut a ripe tomato into two and sprinkle a teaspoon of sugar on each piece to leave overnight in a refrigerator. Eat this first thing in the morning for at least a month. You will find increase in your haemoglobin content.
- Blanch parsley leaves and drink.
- Eat baked lentils.
- Drink two to three cups of cabbage juice daily.
- Blanch nettle leaves and drink three to four cups daily.
- Eat plenty of dates.

50

Bacterial Vaginitis

The vagina acts like a magnet for attracting trouble. If negligent, it can become a breeding ground for bacteria and other obnoxious germs during the hot, humid weather. In vaginal infection, some signs include:
- Change in colour of vaginal discharge.
- Pain during urination.
- Fishy odour with a greyish discharge from the vagina, especially after sexual intercourse.
- At times, light bleeding may occur.

Home Remedies

- Boil parsley in water, strain and drink.
- Garlic can be eaten because of its anti-fungal properties or if applied directly on the vagina.
- The calendula herb controls inflammation.
- Eat plenty of yoghurt.
- Apply yoghurt or a tampon soaked in yoghurt and insert it inside.
- Eat garlic and cabbage in liberal amounts.
- Herbs like black walnut and tea-tree oil are very useful in treating vaginitis.
- Use boric acid dissolved in a little water for douching.
- Drink watermelon juice for increasing urination.
- Soak a teabag in water and cool it in the refrigerator before applying it to the vagina.
- Add 12 teaspoons of calendula to boiling water. Strain and cool it before using for douching.

Home Remedies

- Take a teaspoon of *ajwain* (caraway seeds) and a pinch of salt with water. Repeat after an hour if the white discharge persists.
- Drink cranberry juice daily.

51

Breast Feeding

Many mothers are unable to feed their babies or find it tough to handle. Once the child in delivered, the breasts of the mother feel very hard and the baby may have difficulty in holding the nipple. Problems like nipple soreness, or blocked milk ducts, or breasts painfully engorged with milk, may arise.

Precautions

- If the milk flow is blocked, soap the breast while taking a bath and gently run a wide-toothed comb over it to stimulate milk flow.
- Empty your breasts to the last drop when feeding your baby.
- Increase blood flow towards the nipples by placing a warm flannel on your breast and gently massaging the breast.
- Wear special maternity bras made of cotton.
- Wear a corset to keep the tummy flat.

Home Remedies

- To produce ample milk, drink a glass of beer every day about half an hour before every feed.
- Apply pressure on top of the breast with your thumbs to stimulate the milk flow.
- Grind fennel seeds, dissolve in a cup of boiling water and let it settle down. Drink the water and eat seeds three times a day to obtain more breast milk.
- Drink almond oil for producing more milk.
- Soak buckwheat in milk and add butter before eating.

Home Remedies

- Eat garlic as its flavour affects the flavour of breast milk that appeals to the baby.
- Place a cold flannel on each breast in case of sore nipples.
- For cracked nipples, apply vitamin E oil extracted by breaking a capsule. Olive oil, almond oil or lanolin cream is equally effective.
- Bacteria may occur through cracked nipples and cause infection. Doctors will advise you to take antibiotics. Drink plenty of water to let the infection heal.

52

Female Infertility

Infertility in females refers to the inability to conceive and give birth to a baby. Infertility is different from frigidity where the latter denotes failure to perform the sexual act.

Infertility can be due to the male's sperms not being healthy or sufficient in number to be deposited high up in the women's vagina, or it could be because the women's fallopian tubes are blocked, or her womb is retroverted, or her cervical mucous does not accept the sperms. It could also be due to diseases like gonorrhoea, syphilis, fibroids, chronic anaemia, constipation and leucorrhoea.

It is possible that the couple is not indulging in sex at the time of ovulation. No matter what is the problem, both the man and woman must work together to make things work, for producing a baby is a joint venture.

Precautions

- Avoid smoking as it decreases fertility and increases the risk of miscarriage.
- Restrict alcohol intake as it can impair ejaculation.
- Avoid coffee and cola drinks as caffeine can restrict fertility.
- Cut down on your hectic schedule and avoid stressful jobs.
- Avoid antihistamines like Ibuprofen or aspirin when trying to get pregnant.
- Neither be too thin nor too heavy, if you wish to conceive.
- Snug-fitting underwear or tight denim jeans trap heat and reduce the number of healthy sperm produced by the testicles.
- Avoid hot baths and sauna.
- Douching should be avoided as it alters the acid-alkali balance, making the environment less hospitable for sperm entry.

Home Remedies

- Tender roots of banyan tree should be dried and powdered. At least 20 gms of this is mixed with 20 times its weight of milk and taken for three consecutive nights after the monthly periods are over. No food should be taken for a short while following this intake. This step should be repeated every month after the completion of every menstrual cycle till conception occurs.
- Certain nutrients, especially vitamin C and E, and minerals like zinc prove helpful in countering sterility.
- The herb, winter cherry, should be dried, powdered and taken with milk for five or six nights after menstruation.
- Leaves of *jambul* fruit should be allowed to steep in boiling water. After straining, take the infusion with honey or buttermilk.
- Your diet should contain plenty of seeds, nuts, fruits, vegetables, grains and milk products.
- Certain *yoga asanas* done under the supervision of a trained instructor facilitate conception.
- A wet underwear under a woollen underwear should be worn to improve internal circulation.
- Mud packs may be applied to the abdomen and sexual organs or a cold hipbath taken by sitting in a tub as these are found helpful.

53 Frigidity

This word really applies to lack of sexual response in the female partner or lack of sexual drive. Anxiety about performance is a major turn off in the sexual act. Too much anxiety about the physical act rather than the emotional bonding can lead to problems in the bed.

Further, if the male spouse is tired or stressed out, or worried, it can affect his libido. Conflicts within the relationship can turn off the spouse as resentment can create problems in the bed. Other causes of frigidity could be sexual abuse during childhood, domination of parents, fear of pregnancy, diabetes, hypertension and multiple sclerosis. However a counsellor's advice should be sought if one is unable to talk frankly with the spouse.

Precautions

- A good nutritive diet can counter frigidity.
- Try to make life interesting by taking pleasure trips.

Home Remedies

- Take the anti-stress Ayurvedic drug called *Ashwagandha lehyam* thrice a day with a cup of warm milk.
- Another Ayurveda capsule, called the *Trasina*, taken with water or milk for a month helps control frigidity.

Leucorrhoea

The female vagina, if itchy, smelly or painful, can be a cause of embarrassment and for which certain preventive measures need to be taken. As girls step into puberty, blood flow to the uterus increases as it does also during pregnancy. In most women, a temporary increase in the vaginal fluid occurs at the time the ovary releases the egg. This can happen a week before the next period is due.

Leucorrhoea can be due to 'trichomonal vaginitis' when a yellowish discharge accompanied with itching occurs. Diabetic or pregnant women, or women on oral contraceptive pills, get 'monilial vaginitis'. 'cervicitis' is another form of leucorrhoea where the discharge is accompanied with back pain.

Precautions

Avoid non-vegetarian food till the infection besets you.

Home Remedies

Eat plenty of green leafy vegetables, milk and *ghee* (clarified butter).

A cold hipbath thrice a day is very soothing.

Soak a few fenugreek seeds overnight and next morning add water. Drink after straining it. Add honey if so desired.

A decoction of the bark of *lodhra* is good for douching.

Take 20 gms of *Triphala* powder and mix in 20 litres of water. Boil for 15 minutes. Strain it to use as a douche when the water is lukewarm.

Amalaki seeds boiled with two to three teaspoons of honey will relieve the discharge.

Home Remedies

Put five drops of sandalwood powder in warm water and douche.

Tender leaves of guava are helpful in treating leucorrhoea.

A decoction of fresh walnut leaves boiled in water and strained can be used for douching.

Wear only cotton underwear.

Observe personal cleanliness and hygiene.

55 Menopause

A woman, who stops menstruating after the age of 45 or more, is said to be passing through the menopause stage. It is the stage when a whole range of physical and emotional changes occur in a woman.

Her fertility ends and she experiences a variety of uncomfortable symptoms, including hot flashes, night sweats, vaginal dryness, mood swings and sleep problems. Unusually heavy or light periods mark the onset of menopause and the stage in called peri-menopause when her ovaries produce less of the female hormones — oestrogen and progesterone, while ovulation or the release of monthly egg begins to decrease. The later stage of menopause can lead to brittle bones called 'osteoporosis' — a condition for causing fractures and the narrowing down of arteries.

Precautions

Take to exercises like walking, jogging, swimming, cycling, and avoid a sedentary lifestyle.

Stress and strain should be faced bravely.

Swings should be countered by keeping oneself busy and active.

Keep away from tea, coffee, cola drinks, spicy food, and alcohol, if you have hot flashes.

Home Remedies

Since the bones become brittle, plenty of milk and milk products should be included in the diet.

Liquorice, probably known as *Yasti madhu* or *Meethi lakadi* is a natural source of the hormone called oestrogen and should be taken twice a day with milk.

Home Remedies

About 5 gms of Ayurvedic *Ashwagandha* mixed in milk can be taken to check emotional disturbances.

Take 1 ml. of black cohosh, in tincture form, two to four times a day to ward off hot flashes and night sweat. This should be taken regularly for six weeks and then stopped for four weeks and again resumed to follow the same pattern.

Vitamin E tablets can be taken once a week for some time.

Wear cotton clothes to stay cool as menopause causes excessive perspiration.

A lukewarm water-bath helps to curb flashes in some women.

Vigorous exercises help to keep the bones strong.

Chasteberry helps to restore the hormone, progesterone, levels in hot flashes and depression.

Vaginal dryness can be reduced to some extent by taking a water-soluble lubricant like K-Y jelly.

Eat plenty of protein-rich products to prevent loss of calcium from the bones.

Urinary discomfort due to bladder infections can be temporarily eased by drinking plenty of water, which might mean frequent urination but that alone can take away the infection.

Carrot seeds are valuable in menopause.

Soya plant contains phyto-oestrogens which release the oestrogen necessary for female reproductive organs. So eat soya products.

Menstruation

Many women find it unnatural and experience discomfort a few days before the onset of periods. Mild cramps, headache, mood swings, irritability, depression, anxiety, bloating, chest pain and weight gain are some of the common symptoms. These usually occur due to hormonal fluctuation in a woman's monthly cycle. There is a drop in the production of the hormone called progesterone, which causes the body to retain salt and water a few days before the onset of menstruation. An imbalance between progesterone and oestrogen leads to emotional symptoms like anxiety, depression, etc. All this should be taken in one's stride as it is nature's way of telling you that you are a young and complete woman now.

Precautions

Do not take food that causes constipation.

Vegetables like potato and brinjal should be avoided.

Garlic should be taken to prevent gas formation.

Home Remedies

Crush the leafy pulp of aloe vera and extract the juice. Take five teaspoons of the juice with two teaspoons of honey twice a day for long-lasting relief from pre-menstrual syndrome.

Take the cold infusion of lemon grass and black pepper.

Ajwain (caraway seeds) taken with *gur* (jaggery) and warm water twice or thrice per day provide relief from pain.

Home Remedies

Exercise has a positive effect on the hormonal balance in the body.

hing (asafoetida) in *ghee* or butter in a teaspoon can be taken with a rice bolus. This is followed with a glass of hot water to find relief from painful periods.

Nine or 10 gms powdered sesame seeds can be taken four times a day during menstruation.

In case of excessive bleeding, mix pomegranate leaves with grains of rice and crush in water to make a paste. Take twice daily to curb bleeding.

Amla (Indian gooseberry) is useful is controlling bleeding.

In case of cramps during menstruation, take cramp bark (available at health shops) and make tea with one teaspoon bark in one cup of water.

Camomile tea has anti-spasmodic properties to open out your uterus. Take two or four teaspoons of it in warm water.

Ginger tea with one teaspoon of fresh root ginger in a cup of boiling water is another remedy.

To curb bloating, cut down on salt intake and take vitamin b.

Eat diuretic foods like asparagus, celery, garlic, watercress and parsley.

Take a hot-water bath.

Eat high-fibre food to remove excess oestrogen out of the body, for e.g. barley, oats, vegetables and beans.

Take calcium, milk and bananas as they reduce cramps and mood swings.

Oedema/Water Retention

Oedema means 'swelling of the body parts due to water retention'. It is accumulation of excessive fluids in cells or cavities of the body. The swelling is sometimes localised to the face, legs, abdomen and feet. Oedema is not a disease but an indication that something is wrong in the body. It slows down the healing process and increases the chances of skin infection, faulty blood circulation, thyroid problem, liver disease, kidney problem and anaemia. When the swelling is pressed, it creates a hollow, which does not disappear immediately.

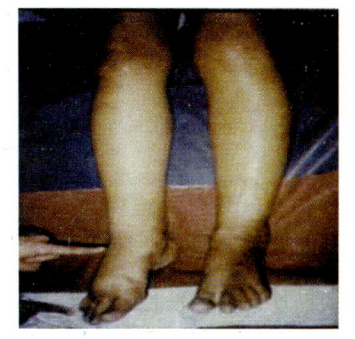

Diuretics are given to cause the body to excrete excess fluid.

Precautions

Avoid salt, fried food and curd.

Eat ripe papaya regularly.

Excess of fat should be avoided.

Desist from sleeping during the day.

Home Remedies

Massage with cow's urine over the affected part of the body.

Mix pepper powder with the juice of *bel* leaves and take three times daily.

Warm mustard oil and apply on the affected part.

Home Remedies

Apple cider vinegar helps to reduce excess fluid.

Eat protein and fat-rich food but avoid salt and carbohydrates as they have more water content.

Exercise regularly to get rid of excessive fluid in body cells and cavities.

Keep the feet slightly raised above the floor with the help of a cushion.

About 10-15 mls. of castor oil should be taken twice by mixing in a cup of warm milk.

Take more potassium through fruits and vegetables like bananas, avocados, potatoes, oranges, meat, poultry, milk and yoghurt.

Drink two to four cups of dandelion tea daily as dandelion is a natural diuretic, allowing the kidneys to drain away excess water.

Make a paste of lotus flower with milk and take thrice daily.

Drink nettle tea by placing a teaspoon of nettle in cold water and boiling for a minute. Strain and cool before drinking.

Put a teaspoon of dried corn silk in cold water. Boil and strain. Drink several times a day.

Eat celery, watermelon, asparagus and cucumber.

As turmeric has anti-inflammatory qualities, eat it liberally to inhibit water retention.

Do a gentle self-massage of your lower legs.

If water retention occurs before you menstruate, take vitamin B6 as it helps to excrete more urine and balances you oestrogen and progesterone levels. Eat plenty of spinach, fish, chickpeas, avocados and bananas. The recommended intake of vitamin B6 is 1.2 mg per day for women. Fluid retention is due to the fluctuating hormone levels that change the function of blood vessels and lymph glands.

Pregnancy Problems

Childbirth is a spectacular natural phenomenon but certain rules are to be observed so that all goes well. Conception is normally followed by morning sickness, particularly in the first trimester. At the same time, problems like heartburn, swollen feet, varicose veins, sleeplessness, back pain, stretch marks also dog the mother's footsteps. As the baby grows inside the mother's womb, the extra weight causes pain and fluid retention in which the feet swell first. At times varicose veins appear along with stretch marks on the stomach and breasts.

First of all, an expectant mother should keep happy to be creating a part of her own. There are certain measures to be adopted for passing through this rather strenuous period.

Home Remedies

- Religiously do some exercises in the early morning hours and go for walks late at night after taking your meal.
- Take short naps during the day to rest your tired back and feet. Place some pillows under your feet when sleeping, as keeping the feet higher than the heart will ease pressure on the feet.
- If the feet ache, place them in a bucket of hot water followed by cold water, thus alternating after every few minutes.
- The growing baby puts pressure on your stomach and acids are forced up into the oesophagus, which can cause a burning sensation. To counter this, eat small meals a number of times and try not to bend.
- Avoid foods like coffee, citrus juices, tomato products, fried food and alcohol.
- Avoid standing for long periods.

Home Remedies

When sitting on a desk or table, keep your feet on a footstool to avoid swelling in the feet.

Keep your weight under control.

Wear maternity tights to keep away varicose veins.

Keep a cold compress on your legs to prevent varicose veins from appearing.

Increase intake of fibrous food, particularly of bread, cereals, flaxseeds, vegetables, broccoli, fruits, nuts, etc. to keep constipation at bay.

Male Problems

There are some physical problems, which are exclusive to the male species and which need treatment. Home remedies are effective in the initial stages but in severe cases, medical advice has to be sought.

59

Erectile Dysfunction

Sex is a part of productive life and is a basic human instinct. Both physical and mental factors affect the ability of man to achieve erection. The most common reason for this failure in psychological. He may be overtired, stressed out, anxious, worried or lacking in self-confidence. All these demand extra consideration, sympathy and love from his spouse or partner. Anger, fear, guilt or any other negative feeling can aggravate the condition. At times, excessive intake of alcohol or cigarette smoking can lead to impotence, causing erection failure or short-lived erection.

Erection is the final point of a complex chain of events. The brain sends signals to the genitals, the blood vessels dilate and the penis gets engorged. When a man cannot get or keep the erection, the problem becomes impotence or erectile dysfunction.

Home Remedies

Take fish oil or flaxseed oil as it improves blood flow and prevents blood vessels from narrowing.

Take evening primrose oil three times a day as it promotes blood vessel health.

Take a capsule of arginine to improve blood flow to the penis.

Exercise helps keep off excess weight, boosts energy and reduces stress.

Aerobic exercise, walking, jogging, swimming or playing tennis is advised.

Avoid cycling because too much riding on the wrong saddle can damage the nerves and blood vessels in the area you sit on.

Garlic is a powerful aphrodisiac and keeps a man fertile. About five or six garlic cloves should be added to a glass of water, boiled till it is half in quantity. Filter, add sugar and take twice a day.

Home Remedies

Dried dates also act like an aphrodisiac and should be taken daily.

Black raisins are very healthy.

Certain *yoga asanas* like *Sarvangasana* and *Dhanurasana* are to be practiced.

An energetic massage all over the body is useful.

An Ayurvedic oil, called Sir Gopala *tailam* should be applied over the pelvic region and massaged.

Take vitamin C as it helps the blood vessels to remain flexible, allowing them to widen and facilitate blood flow.

Take plenty of rest and relaxation to get over anxiety and stress.

Meditation too helps to soothe the nerves by focusing on inhaling and exhaling.

60

Prostate Enlargement

This is part of the aging process in males over 60 years of age. The prostate is the male sex gland about the size of a chestnut. It is made up of a cluster of glands around the urethra at the point where it leaves the bladder. During long years of life, nodules develop in the tissues and enlarge the gland. As the gland enlarges, it narrows the diameter of the urethra and impedes the flow of urine. As a result, the male has to urinate often at night and during the day. Even after urinating, one feels there is incomplete evacuation.

If pressure is put to urinate, blood may pass, cystitis may develop and blood may flow drop by drop. In severe cases, surgery has to be done.

Home Remedies

Two pills of Ayurvedic medicine *Chandraprabhavati* can be taken with milk twice a day.

Shilajit is another Ayurvedic medicine that is effective in solving urinary problems.

Green bananas should be cooked as a vegetable.

Pomegranate is very useful.

Amla powder can be taken twice daily.

Calories

Daily requirement of calories :

For men	: 2200 to 3400
For women	: 1900 to 2800

CALORIES PER 100 GRAMS OF DIFFERENT ITEMS

Name of the food stuff	Calories	Name of the food stuff	Calories
Wheat (whole)	344	Bathua leaves	30
Wheat flour (whole)	341	Methi leaves	49
Wheat sprouts	397	Mustard leaves	34
Rice	354	Peas	104
Maize	363	Beet root	45
Bajra	361	Cauliflower	33
Gram (whole)	338	Cucumber	12
Green Mung	324	Gourd	28
Dried pea	337	Onion	36
Lobia bean	323	Radish	18
Bean	346	Tomato	29
Soyabean	382	Turnip	34
Almond	657	Potato	75
Cashew nut	590	Sweet potato	114
Ground nut	579	Carrot	33
Spinach	48	Fresh mushroom	13
Lettuce	19	Apple	61

Name of the food stuff	Calories
Apricot	36
Lemon, lime, grapefruit and other citrus fruits	37
Orange, Malt	53
Banana	116
Dried dates	303
Fig fresh	85
Fig-dried	269
Grape	76
Guava	58
Lichi	71
Mango	63
Musk melon	26
Papaya	39
Peach	56
Pear	59
Pineapple	57
Plum	45
Pomegranate	77
Hydrogenated oil	900

Name of the food stuff	Calories
Cow milk fresh	64
Cow milk skimmed	34
Cow milk condensed	317
Cheese from skimmed milk	87
Fish, fresh water	95
Fish dried	309
Lamb meat	249
Pork	535
Poultry meat	139
Honey	286
Sugar white	400
Khandasari	389
Cane juice	73
Jam	260
Garlic	139
Tamarind	304
Black pepper	347
Red pepper	291
Clove	293